PREPARING TODAY'S STUDENTS FOR TOMORROW'S JOBS: A DISCUSSION ON CAREER AND TECHNICAL EDUCATION AND TRAINING PROGRAMS

HEARING

BEFORE THE

SUBCOMMITTEE ON EARLY CHILDHOOD, ELEMENTARY, AND SECONDARY EDUCATION

COMMITTEE ON EDUCATION AND THE WORKFORCE

U.S. HOUSE OF REPRESENTATIVES

ONE HUNDRED THIRTEENTH CONGRESS

FIRST SESSION

HEARING HELD IN WASHINGTON, DC, SEPTEMBER 20, 2013

Serial No. 113–34

Printed for the use of the Committee on Education and the Workforce

Available via the World Wide Web:
http://www.gpoaccess.gov/congress/house/education/index.html
or
Committee address: *http://edworkforce.house.gov*

U.S. GOVERNMENT PRINTING OFFICE

WASHINGTON : 2013

82–793 PDF

For sale by the Superintendent of Documents, U.S. Government Printing Office
Internet: bookstore.gpo.gov   Phone: toll free (866) 512–1800; DC area (202) 512–1800
Fax: (202) 512–2104   Mail: Stop IDCC, Washington, DC 20402–0001

D1417948

COMMITTEE ON EDUCATION AND THE WORKFORCE

JOHN KLINE, Minnesota, *Chairman*

Thomas E. Petri, Wisconsin
Howard P. "Buck" McKeon, California
Joe Wilson, South Carolina
Virginia Foxx, North Carolina
Tom Price, Georgia
Kenny Marchant, Texas
Duncan Hunter, California
David P. Roe, Tennessee
Glenn Thompson, Pennsylvania
Tim Walberg, Michigan
Matt Salmon, Arizona
Brett Guthrie, Kentucky
Scott DesJarlais, Tennessee
Todd Rokita, Indiana
Larry Bucshon, Indiana
Trey Gowdy, South Carolina
Lou Barletta, Pennsylvania
Martha Roby, Alabama
Joseph J. Heck, Nevada
Susan W. Brooks, Indiana
Richard Hudson, North Carolina
Luke Messer, Indiana

George Miller, California,
  Senior Democratic Member
Robert E. Andrews, New Jersey
Robert C. "Bobby" Scott, Virginia
Rubén Hinojosa, Texas
Carolyn McCarthy, New York
John F. Tierney, Massachusetts
Rush Holt, New Jersey
Susan A. Davis, California
Raúl M. Grijalva, Arizona
Timothy H. Bishop, New York
David Loebsack, Iowa
Joe Courtney, Connecticut
Marcia L. Fudge, Ohio
Jared Polis, Colorado
Gregorio Kilili Camacho Sablan,
  Northern Mariana Islands
John A. Yarmuth, Kentucky
Frederica S. Wilson, Florida
Suzanne Bonamici, Oregon

Juliane Sullivan, *Staff Director*
Jody Calemine, *Minority Staff Director*

———

SUBCOMMITTEE ON EARLY CHILDHOOD, ELEMENTARY, AND SECONDARY EDUCATION

TODD ROKITA, Indiana, *Chairman*

John Kline, Minnesota
Thomas E. Petri, Wisconsin
Virginia Foxx, North Carolina
Kenny Marchant, Texas
Duncan Hunter, California
David P. Roe, Tennessee
Glenn Thompson, Pennsylvania
Martha Roby, Alabama
Susan W. Brooks, Indiana

Carolyn McCarthy, New York,
  Ranking Minority Member
Robert C. "Bobby" Scott, Virginia
Susan A. Davis, California
Raúl M. Grijalva, Arizona
Marcia L. Fudge, Ohio
Jared Polis, Colorado
Gregorio Kilili Camacho Sablan,
  Northern Mariana Islands
Frederica S. Wilson, Florida

CONTENTS

PREPARING TODAY'S STUDENTS FOR TOMORROW'S JOBS: A DISCUSSION ON CAREER AND TECHNICAL EDUCATION AND TRAINING PROGRAMS

Friday, September 20, 2013
U.S. House of Representatives
Subcommittee on Early Childhood,
Elementary, and Secondary Education
Committee on Education and the Workforce
Washington, DC

The subcommittee met, pursuant to call, at 10:01 a.m., in room 2175, Rayburn House Office Building, Hon. Todd Rokita [chairman of the subcommittee] presiding.

Present: Representatives Rokita, Kline, Roe, Thompson, Brooks, Davis, and Grijalva.

Staff Present: Katherine Bathgate, Deputy Press Secretary; James Bergeron, Director of Education and Human Services Policy; Heather Couri, Deputy Director of Education and Human Services Policy; Amy Raaf Jones, Education Policy Counsel and Senior Advisor; Rosemary Lahasky, Professional Staff Member; Krisann Pearce, General Counsel; Dan Shorts, Legislative Assistant; Nicole Sizemore, Deputy Press Secretary; Alex Sollberger, Communications Director; Alissa Strawcutter, Deputy Clerk; Brad Thomas, Senior Education Policy Advisor; Tylease Alli, Minority Clerk/Intern and Fellow Coordinator; Jeremy Ayers, Minority Education Policy Advisor; Kelly Broughan, Minority Education Policy Associate; Jody Calemine, Minority Staff Director; Jacque Chevalier, Minority Education Policy Advisor; Tiffany Edwards, Minority Press Secretary for Education; Jamie Fasteau, Minority Director of Education Policy; Liz Hollis, Minority Special Assistant to Staff Director; Eunice Ikene, Minority Staff Assistant; and Megan O'Reilly, Minority General Counsel.

Chairman ROKITA. Good morning. A quorum being present, the subcommittee will come to order. Thank you for joining us today for our hearing to discuss career and technical education training programs under the Carl D. Perkins Career and Technical Education Act. I would like to send a warm welcome to our witnesses whose testimony will be invaluable to our efforts to reauthorize and strengthen the law.

The Perkins Act provides Federal funding to States to support career and technical education or what we call in the business CTE

(1)

programs. These programs offer high school and community college students the opportunity to gain the skills and experience necessary to compete for jobs in a broad range of fields, including health care, transportation, construction, hospitality, and that is just to name a few.

A number of state school districts and post-secondary institutions have implemented truly exceptional CTE programs. In Massachusetts, for example, Worcester—I am sure I am mispronouncing that being from the Midwest—Technical High School has partnered with Tufts University to provide affordable animal care for low-income families. The university funds a resident veterinarian to operate an onsite clinic at the high school, and the tech students get to work at the clinic and obtain hands-on experience. We are fortunate to have with us the principal who will share more information about this initiative during her testimony.

To prepare our students for high demand jobs in my home State of Indiana, Ivy Tech's Ivy Institute of Technology offers automotive, manufacturing, welding, and other specialized training programs that allow students to learn new career skills in just 40 weeks. In Wisconsin, Gateway Technical College offers more than 60 career education programs, including a medical assistant degree program that provides students with real world clinical, administrative, and laboratory training.

However, despite these shining examples, the Bureau of Labor Statistics recently reported more than 8 million Americans between the ages of 16 and 24 are still looking for jobs. By strengthening the career and technical education programs funded under the Perkins Act, we can help. We can help more of these young people gain an edge in the workforce.

As we begin our discussions on improving the act we must first assess the Federal role in career and technical education. To receive funding through the act States with CTE programs must comply with a series of Federal reporting requirements, some of which are duplicative to those under the Workforce Investment Act and the Elementary and Secondary Education Act. We cannot allow redundant Federal mandates to make it harder for States to offer the career training opportunities that young people need.

We must also discuss ways to ensure CTE programs are actually effective. States and schools must have the flexibility to coordinate with the local business community to develop and implement programs that prepare students for in-demand jobs. Additionally, CTE course work should provide students with opportunities to obtain relevant certificates, credits, and hands-on experience that will allow them to more seamlessly integrate into the workforce.

Recognizing the success of CTE programs depends upon effective teachers. We must examine ways to help states recruit and retain educators with valuable technical knowledge and experience. A 2010 study released by the National Association of State Directors of Career Technical Education Consortium identified dozens of States that are struggling to attract CTE teachers in several key career sectors, including health sciences, manufacturing, agriculture, and the rapidly growing STEM fields.

As we work to rebuild our economy after the recent recession, strengthening career and technical education programs will help put more Americans on the path to a prosperous future. In the coming weeks this committee will discuss a range of proposals to improve the Perkins Act, including those offered in President Obama's Blueprint to Transform Career and Technical Education, and I look forward to beginning that discussion right now.

Once again, I would like to thank our panel of witnesses for joining us. And I would now yield to my distinguished colleague from Arizona, Raul Grijalva, for his opening remarks.

[The statement of Chairman Rokita follows:]

Prepared Statement of Hon. Todd Rokita, Chairman, Subcommittee on Early Childhood, Elementary, and Secondary Education

The Perkins Act provides federal funding to states to support career and technical education (or CTE) programs. These programs offer high school and community college students the opportunity to gain the skills and experience necessary to compete for jobs in a broad range of fields, including health care, transportation, construction, and hospitality, just to name a few.

A number of states, school districts, and postsecondary institutions have implemented truly exceptional CTE programs. In Massachusetts, Worcester Technical High School has partnered with Tufts University to provide affordable animal care for low-income families. The university funds a resident veterinarian to operate an on-site clinic at the high school, and Worcester Tech students get to work at the clinic and obtain hands-on experience. We are fortunate to have with us today the principal of Worcester Tech who will share more information about this initiative during her testimony.

To prepare students for high-demand jobs in my home state of Indiana, Ivy Tech's Ivy Institute of Technology offers automotive, manufacturing, welding, and other specialized training programs that allow students to learn new career skills in just 40 weeks. And in Wisconsin, Gateway Technical College offers more than 60 career education programs, including a Medical Assistant degree program that provides students with real-world clinical, administrative, and laboratory training.

However, despite these shining examples, the Bureau of Labor Statistics recently reported more than 8 million Americans between the ages of 16 and 24 are still looking for jobs. By strengthening the career and technical education programs funded under the Perkins Act, we can help more of these young people gain an edge in the workforce.

As we begin our discussions on improving the Perkins Act, we must first assess the federal role in career and technical education. To receive funding through the Perkins Act, states with CTE programs must comply with a series of federal reporting requirements, some of which are duplicative to those under the Workforce Investment Act and the Elementary and Secondary Education Act. We cannot allow redundant federal mandates to make it harder for states to offer the career training opportunities our young people need.

We must also discuss ways to ensure CTE programs are effective. States and schools must have the flexibility to coordinate with the local business community to develop and implement programs that prepare students for in-demand jobs. Additionally, CTE coursework should provide students with opportunities to obtain relevant certificates, credits, and hands-on experience that will allow them to more seamlessly integrate into the workforce or get ahead in their quest to earn a postsecondary degree.

Recognizing the success of CTE programs depends upon effective teachers, we must examine ways to help states recruit and retain educators with valuable technical knowledge and experience. A 2010 study released by the National Association of State Directors of Career Technical Education Consortium identified dozens of states that are struggling to attract CTE teachers in several key career sectors, including health sciences, manufacturing, agriculture, and the rapidly-growing STEM fields.

As we work to rebuild our economy after the recent recession, strengthening career and technical education programs will help put more Americans on the path to a prosperous future. In the coming weeks, this committee will discuss a range of proposals to improve the Perkins Act, including those offered in President Obama's "Blueprint to Transform Career and Technical Education," and I look forward to beginning that discussion today.

Mr. GRIJALVA. Thank you very much, Mr. Chairman, and thank you for the hearing. And I agree it is important to initiate this discussion about this very important component of education in our country. Today's hearing will showcase innovations in delivery of career and technical education programs, many of which are funded under the Carl D. Perkins Career and Technical Education Improvement Act of 2006.

Career technical education programs prepare millions of Americans to succeed in both college and career, and gives them access to modern job skills they need and that employers are demanding. This act has supported the development of academic and career and technical skills among secondary and post-secondary education students of all backgrounds. Helping to prepare them for in-demand and high-paying jobs is the goal.

High quality, relevant, and rigorous CTE is imperative for our Nation to stay competitive and to build a stronger economy. By ensuring that students not only graduate from high school college- and career-ready, but also succeed in college and the global economy, we are in that way securing our Nation's future. Of the 30 fastest growing occupations, about two-thirds require post-secondary education or training and that need is projected to grow over the next years. In the State of Arizona there are currently 70 CTE programs with over 229,000 students enrolled, of which 30 percent are Latino and over 40 percent of those students are of color.

In Arizona investment in CTE programs has diminished. After the harmful sequestration cuts, public funding for CTE is at a historic low despite our State consistently performing well on indicators of student success. We shouldn't cut funding from programs that mean the difference between getting ahead and falling behind for workers all over this Nation. We should support quality programs that allow students to explore different career interests and work-based learning opportunities that help prepare them for both the workforce and further post-secondary education. We know there is a skills gap, we know career technical education is integral to closing that gap.

Evaluations of career academies across the country have demonstrated that offering students academically rigorous curricula embedded in career-related programs can reduce high school dropout rates and prepare students for high-earning, high-skilled careers. High school students who graduate from career academies make on the average 11 percent more per year than the non-career academy counterparts. One in four who earn a post-secondary certificate eventually earn a 4-year college degree. Higher earnings help our overall economy, increasing consumer spending and strengthening and growing the middle class.

I welcome our distinguished panel of witnesses, as they have some of the most extensive insights into these programs. We are grateful they are sharing their knowledge. And I look forward to continued collaboration with the majority to address reauthorization of this very vital and important program.

With that, Mr. Chairman, I yield back, and thank you.

Chairman ROKITA. Thank you Mr. Grijalva.

[The statement of Mr. Grijalva follows:]

Prepared Statement of Hon. Raúl M. Grijalva, a Representative in Congress From the State of Arizona

Good morning and thank you, Chairman Rokita.

Today's hearing will showcase innovations in delivery of career and technical education programs, many of which are funded under the Carl D. Perkins Career and Technical Education Improvement Act of 2006.

Career technical education programs prepare millions of Americans to succeed in both college and career and gives them access to the modern job skills they need and that employers demand. This act has supported the development of academic and career and technical skills among secondary and postsecondary education students of all backgrounds; helping to prepare them for in-demand and high paying jobs. High quality, relevant, and rigorous CTE is imperative for our nation to stay competitive and build a stronger economy. By ensuring that students not only graduate from high school, college- and career-ready, but also succeed in college and the global economy, we are securing our nation's future.

Of the 30 fastest-growing occupations, about two-thirds require postsecondary education or training and projected to grow over the years. In the state of Arizona, there are currently 70 CTE programs with over 229,569 students enrolled, of which 30% are Hispanic students.

In Arizona, investment in CTE programs has diminished. After the harmful sequestration cuts, public funding for CTE is at historic lows, despite our state consistently performing on indicators of student success. We shouldn't cut funding for programs that mean the difference between getting ahead and falling behind for workers all over the country. We should support quality programs that allow students to explore different career interests and work-based learning opportunities that help prepare them for both the workforce and further postsecondary education. We know there's a skills gap. We know Career technical education is integral to closing that gap.

Evaluations of career academies across the country have demonstrated that offering students academically rigorous curricula embedded in career-related programs can reduce high school drop-out rates and prepare students for high-earning and high-skilled careers.

• High school students who graduate from career academies make on average 11 percent more per year than their non-career academy counterparts.

• One in four who earn a postsecondary certificate eventually earn a four-year college degree.

• Higher earnings help our overall economy, increasing consumer spending and strengthening the middle class.

I welcome our distinguished panel of witnesses, as they have some of the most extensive insights into these programs, we are grateful they are sharing their knowledge. And I look forward to continued collaboration with the Majority to address reauthorization of this important program.

————

Chairman ROKITA. Pursuant to Committee Rule 7(c), all subcommittee members will be permitted to submit written statements to be included in the permanent hearing record. And without objection, the hearing record will remain open for 14 days to allow statements, questions for the record, and other extraneous material referenced during the hearing to be submitted into the official record.

I just would like to remind members, if and when we adjourn early, that as usual they may submit questions for the record. And I say that because we are not sure when votes will come today. They may come as early as 10:30 or so. If that is the case we will have to adjourn, the hearing will not be returning. The witnesses are nodding yes like they have heard that story before.

So thank you, and appreciate you all coming again.

It is now my pleasure to introduce our distinguished panel of witnesses. Mr. Alvin Bargas is the president of the Pelican Chapter of Associated Builders and Contractors. He has been an active participant in ABC since 1979, first as a volunteer member, then chairman of the Pelican Chapter, and a member of the chapter national board of directors.

Dr. Sheila Harrity is the principal of Worcester Technical High School—I am teachable—the largest of seven high schools in the city of Worcester, Massachusetts. She was most recently selected as the Massachusetts principal of the year for 2014 and as the MetLife National Association of Secondary School Principals 2014 national principal of year.

Welcome to both of you.

Next we have Mr. John Fischer, who is the deputy commissioner for transformation and innovation at the Vermont Agency of Education. Mr. Fischer has previously held positions at Plymouth State University and in the New Hampshire Community College System. He currently serves as president of the National Association of State Directors of Career Technical Education Consortium.

Mr. Fischer, welcome.

And Mr. Frank Britt is the chief executive officer at Penn Foster, Incorporated. He also currently serves as the operating advisor at Bain Capital Ventures. He has over 20 years of experience focused on helping grow companies in the education, media, technology, industrial, and consumer goods industries, including a variety of senior-level positions at IBM and Accenture.

Welcome, Mr. Britt.

Before I recognize each of you to provide your testimony explain let me briefly explain our lighting system, and really that is sometimes more for us up here than you there. You will each have 5 minutes to present your testimony. When you begin the light in front of you will turn green, when 1 minute is left it will turn yellow, when your time has expired the light will turn red. At that point I ask you to wrap up your remarks as best as you are able.

After everyone has testified, members here will each have 5 minutes to ask questions of the panel. And with that I would now like to recognize Mr. Bargas for 5 minutes.

Sir.

STATEMENT OF ALVIN BARGAS, PRESIDENT, PELICAN CHAPTER, ASSOCIATED BUILDERS & CONTRACTORS, INC.

Mr. BARGAS. Thank you, Chairman Rokita, Congressman Grijalva, and members of the Subcommittee on Early Childhood, Elementary, and Secondary Education. My name is Alvin Bargas, and I serve as president of Associated Builders and Contractors, Pelican Chapter, located in Baton Rouge, Louisiana. The Pelican Chapter's volunteer leaders are committed to training a safe and highly skilled construction workforce. The chapter offers construction craft education programs at its Baton Rouge and Lake Charles training centers to currently more than 1,900 students.

Since 1983, ABC member companies and industry-related partners have funded more than $43 million in training costs. ABC has partnership agreements with 43 high schools in 17 districts, which includes 76 classes with more than 1,100 students per year in demand crafts such as welding and pipe fitting. We also engage high school students through craft competitions in a 3-day Build Your Future event. In addition to funding, ABC members alone donate more than $50,000 per year in materials and equipment and volunteer 1,600 hours-plus annually in the classrooms.

Louisiana's construction industry now faces a workforce challenge. Project announcements in excess of $60 billion in new construction, plus the expansion of existing facilities, is driving the need for skilled workers. Retirements, career changes, et cetera, will drive demand for an additional 51,300 workers. Even with an exploding workforce demand for skilled construction workforce, public high schools continue to focus on 4-year college prep curriculums. While this pathway is important, students should be offered opportunities to learn skills that prepare them for high-paying, in-demand careers that do not require a Bachelors degree.

That said, the expansion of career and technical education options should never come at the expense of academic rigor or quality instruction and must clearly align with industry needs and post-secondary credentials. ABC and its partners are leading the charge to align our education system with future workforce demands. Construction industry and education stakeholders established a Craft Workforce Development Taskforce which created a strategic road map entitled ''Building Louisiana's Craft Workforce.''

The task force has ensured that an industry-recognized and academically rigorous construction CTE curriculum will be consistently delivered across Louisiana's training providers. The Louisiana Community and Technical College System and the Louisiana Department of Education have adopted the curriculum of the NCCER, which blends classroom instruction with hands-on training that articulates to post-secondary credential and community college programs. The training providers are focused on leveraging capacity at high schools, as well as leveraging assets such as facilities and funding with private providers. Training delivery includes compressed schedules for industry-based certification and even weekend alternatives.

The Louisiana State Government has also enacted innovative education reforms such as Course Choice, which gives high school students the option to choose from a diverse range of courses, including core academics, college preparation, and career training. Through Course Choice students can customize their learning path by gaining industry-based certifications in addition to earning high school and college credits. The program provides all Louisiana students equal access to career training and a head start on a post-secondary credential and ultimately a career.

Course Choice can serve as a catalyst to recruit and train capable young people to either step into higher wage construction jobs or continue on to complete post-secondary courses. To achieve this, Course Choice provides that students, parents, and school counselors collaborate to make sure students register in courses that are appropriate for their age, interest, and capabilities. As a Course Choice provider, ABC is offering electrical, pipefitting, and welding to 34 students.

Our challenge ahead is to focus our current resources to support CTE programs for in-demand industries that provide students with innovative and flexible training options that stretch from high school to advanced post-secondary credentials. This includes promoting new and existing partnerships between industry, government, and education providers while establishing clear accountability indicators and easily understood measures of success.

On behalf of the Associated Builders and Contractors Pelican Chapter, I would like to thank the committee for holding today's hearing on this very important subject. Thank you.

Chairman ROKITA. Excellent, Mr. Bargas. Thank you.

[The statement of Mr. Bargas follows:]

Prepared Statement of Alvin M. Bargas, President, Associated Builders and Contractors (ABC), Pelican Chapter

CHAIRMAN ROKITA, CONGRESSMAN GRIJALVA, AND MEMBERS OF THE SUB-COMMITTEE ON EARLY CHILDHOOD, ELEMENTARY, AND SECONDARY EDUCATION: Good morning and thank you for the opportunity to testify before you today on "Preparing Today's Students for Tomorrow's Jobs: A Discussion on Career and Technical Education and Training Programs."

My name is Alvin Bargas. I serve as the president of Associated Builders and Contractors (ABC) Pelican Chapter located in Baton Rouge, Louisiana. ABC is a national nonprofit trade association representing 22,000 members from more than 19,000 construction and industry-related firms. Founded on the merit shop philosophy, ABC and its 72 chapters help members develop people, win work and deliver that work safely, ethically, profitably and for the betterment of the communities in which ABC and its members work. The Pelican Chapter has a total membership of 438 companies.

The Pelican Chapter's volunteer leaders are committed to training a safe, highly skilled construction workforce. Education and training will always be a win-win situation for both the employer and the employee. With nationally accredited curricula developed for the construction industry, the Pelican Chapter is training hundreds of men and women in industry-related specialties to meet and exceed the most exacting standards in the country. With the clout and knowledge provided by some of the most qualified instructors in the U.S., ABC trained workers tend to receive higher wages and experience more job satisfaction and greater job retention.

The Pelican Chapter offers construction craft education programs at its Baton Rouge and Lake Charles training centers. Currently, the training centers have a combined enrollment of more than 1,900 high school and adult students. Since 1983, ABC Pelican Chapter member contractors and industry-related partners have privately funded more than $43,000,000 in training costs.

Further, ABC has developed partnership agreements with 43 high schools in 17 school districts. This partnership includes 76 classes with more than 1,100 students per year in high-demand trades such as welding, electrical, carpentry and pipefitting. The Pelican Chapter also engages high school students through craft competitions, tuition-free summer training courses, career counseling and a three-day Build Your Future event that reaches more than 900 students. These achievements would not exist without the committed support of the construction industry. In addition to funding, ABC members alone donate more than $50,000 per year in materials and equipment. More importantly, our members volunteer 1,600 hours per year in classrooms and when students graduate from school, ABC contractors put them to work.

In the wake of hurricanes Katrina and Rita, Louisiana faced a major challenge of recruiting and training a skilled workforce to rebuild the state. In response, ABC brought together construction industry and education stakeholders, including Louisiana Community and Technical College System (LCTCS), Louisiana Department of Education, organized labor, Louisiana Workforce Commission (LWC), Board of Supervisors of Higher Education, as well as industry groups such as the Greater Baton Rouge Industry Alliance, New Orleans Business Roundtable and the Southwest Louisiana Construction Users Council—all of which represent Louisiana's vital refining and petrochemical end users. With ABC's leadership, the coalition's mission was to create a strategy to recruit, train, and retain a safe, skilled and productive construction workforce. This strategy was published in "Recommendations for Confronting the Skilled Construction Workforce Shortage in Louisiana" in October 2006.

Louisiana's construction industry now faces another workforce challenge due to new technologies in the extraction of natural gas and a renaissance in oil refining and chemical production. Project announcements in excess of $60 billion in new construction, plus the expansion of existing facilities is driving the need for skilled workers. The LWC is predicting 35,000 new workers over the next four to five years may be necessary. This challenge will be exacerbated by our aging workforce—an estimated 17 percent of current construction workers nationwide will retire in the next decade. Retirements coupled with career changes, promotions to management, business formations, etc. will drive demand in Louisiana for an additional 51,300 workers, assuming an attrition rate of only 10 percent.

Even with an exploding demand for a skilled construction workforce, most secondary school systems are not structured to deliver a high level of technical education. Public high schools almost exclusively focus on the four-year college prep curriculum for all students. While this pathway is important, students should be offered opportunities to learn skills that prepare them for the many high paying, in-demand careers that do not require a bachelor's degree. That said, the expansion of Career and Technical Education (CTE) options should never come at the expense of academic rigor or quality instruction and must clearly align with industry workforce needs and post-secondary credentials. Louisiana must prepare its young people for success in the classroom and in the workplace.

In Louisiana, ABC and its partners are once again leading the charge to make our education system more closely aligned with future workforce demands. In collaboration with construction industry and education stakeholders and organized labor, a Craft Workforce Development Taskforce (Taskforce) was established. This broad-based Taskforce has created a strategic roadmap titled ''Building Louisiana's Craft Workforce.''

I am pleased to report that we are already making progress in this effort. In a major step forward, the Taskforce has ensured that an industry recognized and academically rigorous construction CTE curriculum will be consistently delivered across Louisiana's training providers. In an effort to bring consistency and transferability to the curriculum that training providers use in the classrooms and labs, the LCTCS and the Louisiana Department of Education have adopted the curriculum of the NCCER, a not-for-profit 501(c)(3) education foundation. This curriculum blends classroom instruction with hands-on training that articulates to post-secondary credential and community college programs.

Aligning industry-recognized curriculum with community and technical colleges, high schools, and ABC allows students and instructors to easily transition from one provider to another depending on personal needs and capacity requirements.

With facilities statewide in strategic locations, the LCTCS serves as the lead training partner. Training providers are focused on leveraging capacity at high schools as well as leveraging assets such as facilities and funding with private providers, which includes ABC and the AFL-CIO. Training schedules have been amended to accommodate varying demand, such as compressed schedules for industry based certifications (NCCER and American Welding Society) and evening and weekend class alternatives.

Training providers are also sharing a pool of instructors that can be deployed to various locations based on need. Web enhancements are being completed by the LCTCS and LWC.

The Louisiana state government also is enacting innovative education reforms that will provide better opportunities for students to access CTE. Louisiana's Governor and state legislators collaborated with the Board of Elementary and Secondary Education (BESE) to create Course Choice, which gives high school students the option to choose from a diverse range of courses—including core academics, college preparation and career training—that are offered by a range of providers.

Through Course Choice, students can customize their learning path to prepare for higher education and careers. The program offers them opportunities to gain industry-based certifications, in addition to earning high school and college credit. Course Choice is an innovative approach to provide all Louisiana students equal access to not only career training, but a head-start on a postsecondary credential and ultimately a career.

ABC believes that innovative reforms like Course Choice can serve as a catalyst to recruit and train capable young people to either step into a higher-wage construction job based on their skills or continue on to complete the post-secondary courses they need to advance in their careers. To achieve this, Course Choice provides that students, parents and school counselors collaborate to make sure students register in courses that are appropriate for their age, interests and capabilities. From approximately 100 applicants, the BESE and the Department of Education selected 21 course providers, including the Pelican Chapter and LCTCS, which reach more than 3,000 Louisiana students. As of August 2013, ABC is offering electrical, pipefitting and welding Course Choice programs and has about 34 students enrolled.

Building America's construction workforce to meet demand is going to require new and innovative ideas, as well as cooperative partnerships among stakeholders from a myriad of public agencies and private entities.

The challenge ahead is to focus our current resources to support CTE programs for in-demand industries that provide students with innovative and flexible training options that stretch from high school to advanced postsecondary credentials. This effort includes promoting new and existing partnerships between industries, government, and education providers while establishing clear accountability indicators and easily understood measures of success.

There is a renaissance in the foundations on which Louisiana delivers career and technical education. It is a renaissance that will touch thousands of Louisiana youth, not to mention underemployed and unemployed adults. We are on the cusp of doing our part to rebuild America's middle class by putting people to work in high paying careers in construction.

On behalf of Associated Builders and Contractors Pelican Chapter, I'd like to thank the subcommittee for holding today's hearing on this important subject. Mr. Chairman, this concludes my formal remarks. I am prepared to answer any questions you and the other members of the subcommittee may have.

———

Chairman ROKITA. Good morning, Dr. Harrity. You are recognized for 5 minutes.

STATEMENT OF SHEILA HARRITY, PRINCIPAL, WORCESTER TECHNICAL HIGH SCHOOL

Ms. HARRITY. Chairman Rokita, Congressman Grijalva, and members of the subcommittee, thank you for inviting me here today to discuss career and technical education and training programs. My name is Sheila Harrity, and I am the proud principal of Worcester Technical High School in Worcester, Mass. I also just received a huge honor of being selected as the 2014 MetLife/NASSP National High School Principal of the Year.

Worcester is the second-largest city in New England, and Worcester Tech is the largest of seven high schools in the city. We have 1,400 students in 24 different technical programs within 4 small learning communities. Sixty-three percent of our students qualify for free or reduced lunch, 19 percent are special ed, and the ethnic backgrounds reflect the city demographics.

Previously Worcester Tech was the lowest-performing high school in our city and one of the poorest-performing vocational schools in our State. Presently we have a 92 percent first-time passing rate in English language arts, 84 percent in math, 96 percent in science, and last year 96.4 percent of our students graduated in 4 years. The achievement gap has decreased significantly and in some groups is nonexistent.

Students are prepared for success with a rigorous curriculum, including a variety of advanced placement courses that combines academic with hands-on experience in school and in the workplace through internship and cooperative educational opportunities. They graduate with all their academic requirements and with industry recognized national certifications. Our students are graduating college and career ready. Eighty-two percent went on to higher education, 13 percent went directly into the world of work, and 2 percent joined the military.

Worcester Tech has over than 350 business and industry advisors that contribute to the direction and success of the school and its students. The advisors consist of representatives of local business and industry related to the programs, organized labor, and postsecondary institutions, parents, guardians, students, and representatives from registered apprenticeship programs. They are integral partners to our program providing direction on training, equipment, certification, licensure, education, and career opportunities. Each technical program works to provide industry-recognized credentials, as well as college credits to expand each student's opportunity for post-secondary success.

Our allied health students graduate with a high school diploma and seven college credits, a certificate in allied health, certification in CPR, first aid, certified nursing assistants, home health aide, and EMT. In our IT program students graduate with up to 18 college credits from Northeastern University, as well as being certified in A+ and a Certified Cisco Networking Associate.

With the assistance of business and higher education partners we receive new equipment at no or reduced cost while the sponsors benefit by having students trained on their latest equipment. A donation from Harr-Toyota has allowed us to create a 16-bay service center furnished and equipped with state-of-the-art automotive technology servicing over 250 vehicles a month.

We are committed to building partnerships with local 2- and 4-year colleges and universities. Our Tufts at Tech animal clinic was created by a school partnership with Tufts University and provides affordable animal care for low-income families in the Worcester area. Tufts University funds a veterinarian to run the clinic and our students work alongside the doctor providing animal care.

Two years ago Worcester Tech became a STEM Career and College Innovation School, which created a pipeline for our students to obtain STEM jobs upon graduation or study STEM-related fields in college. With this 21st century focus we are training students to meet the employment demands of the area's growing biomedical, technology, and manufacturing industries. These partnerships will keep jobs in Worcester for another 100 years and keep our city strong and viable.

Through the leadership efforts of our manufacturing and construction instructors our students worked alongside elite college engineering students from Worcester Polytechnical Institute to develop and build a modular, zero-energy home that competed in the U.S. Department of Energy Solar Decathlon, which was held in Datong, China. This project helped them hone their skills on the latest technologies and their representative fields, and see the fruit of their labors in a truly once-in-a-lifetime global cultural experience.

Successful technical schools require strong links to the community, business and industry, and academic institutions. Our school's success and the city's success are intertwined. Worcester Tech is part of an economic engine coordinating the needs and desires of industry for our highly trained, adaptable workforce with the needs and desires of our students to secure good-paying, rewarding jobs in the field of their choice.

Mr. Rokita, this concludes my prepared testimony, but I would be happy to answer any questions you or other committee members may have. Thank you.

Chairman ROKITA. Thank you, Doctor.

[The statement of Ms. Harrity follows:]

Prepared Statement of Dr. Sheila M. Harrity, Principal, Worcester Technical High School, Worcester, Massachusetts

CHAIRMAN ROKITA, CONGRESSMAN GRIJALVA, AND MEMBERS OF THE SUBCOMMITTEE: Thank you for inviting me here today to discuss career and technical education and training programs. My name is Sheila Harrity and I am the proud principal of Worcester Technical High School in Worcester, Massachusetts. I also just received the huge honor of being selected as the 2014 MetLife/NASSP National High School Principal of the Year and would like to speak on behalf of my fellow middle and high school leaders.

Worcester, Massachusetts is the second largest city in New England. Worcester Technical High School is the largest of seven high schools in the City of Worcester. It has 1400 students in 24 technical programs within four small learning communities. The demographics of Worcester Tech consist of: 53% female, 47% male, 63% qualify for free or reduced lunch, 19% are special needs, ethnic backgrounds reflect the city demographics. Worcester Technical High School has met Adequate Yearly Progress (AYP) for "No Child Left Behind" for five out of the past six years. We exceeded our benchmarks in English, mathematics, and every sub-group. In 2012 and 2013 WTHS also met the Progress and Performance Index (PPI) both in the Annual PPI and the Cumulative PPI.

In the past seven (7) years at Worcester Technical High School, students' Massachusetts Comprehensive Assessment System (MCAS) exam scores have risen significantly. In English Language Arts, 92% of the students scored in the advanced/proficient categories, an increase of 65%, with a less than 1% failure rate. In mathematics, 84% of the students scored in the advanced/proficient categories, an increase of 49%, with a 2% failure rate. In science, 96% of the current 10th and 11th grade students passed with a 4% failure rate. Presently, the Class of 2012 has a 96.4% four year graduation rate with a 1.5% drop out rate.

Massachusetts, as well as other states in our nation, has seen increasing achievement gaps between white students and minority students. At WTHS, the achievement gap has decreased significantly and in some subgroups is non-existent. From 2006-2013, Hispanic students had a 65% gain in ELA and a 49% increase in math. Low-income students showed a 64% gain in ELA and a 50% increase in math. In addition, black students had a 48% gain in ELA and a 32% increase in math.

Recognizing the need for Advanced Placement classes for the students at our school, administration applied for, and was accepted in a grant program associated with the National Math and Science Initiative. The Massachusetts chapter, Mass Insight, helps provide inner city schools with funds for books and supplies, professional development, and student support in an effort to help close the achievement and access gap for many underserved students in the inner city. In 2008, Worcester Tech began the school's entry into Advanced Placement with AP Biology. The school now offers AP Language, AP Literature, AP Statistics, AP Computer Science, AP Environmental Science, AP Physics and AP Calculus. In the past 4 years, Worcester Technical High School has increased student enrollment from 18 students to 183.

Students are prepared for success with a rigorous curriculum that combines academics with hands-on experience, in school and in the workplace, through internships and cooperative education opportunities. They graduate with all academic requirements and with industry-recognized national certifications. Worcester Technical High School graduates are graduating college and career ready. The profile of the 2013 graduates is: 82% went on to higher education, 13% went directly into the world of work, and 2% joined the military.

Guiding the school, WTHS has over 350 industry advisors that contribute to the direction and success of the school and its students. These 350 individuals create both the General Advisory Board and the Program Advisory Committees. The Program Advisory Committees are established for each approved technical program and meet to review the curriculum, equipment, internships/co-ops, and career trends of the respective programs. The program advisory committees consist of representatives of local business and industry related to the program, organized labor, postsecondary institutions, parents/guardians, students, and representatives from registered apprenticeship programs, if applicable. The program advisory committees are integral partners in the provision of a truly college-career ready curriculum. They are the front lines for the industries that they represent. They provide direction to the programs as to the trends in their fields in regards to training, equipment, certifications, licensure, education, and careers. The technical instructors work diligently to both lead the committees and incorporate recommendations.

Each technical program is working towards providing industry recognized credentials as well as college credits to expand each student's opportunities for post secondary success. Two specific examples are: in Allied Health students are graduating with a high school diploma, a certificate in Allied Health, certification in CPR/First Aid, Certified Nursing Assistant (CNA), Home Health Aid, and EMT, which earns them seven college credits; in Information Technology programs students are graduating with up to 18 college credits from Northeastern University, as well as being certified in A+ and as a Certified Cisco Networking Associate (CCNA).

With the assistance of business and higher education partners, entrustments are created to keep the schools' technical programs outfitted with state of the art equipment. Entrustments are mutually beneficial. The school receives new equipment at reduced or no cost while the sponsor benefits by having students trained on their newest equipment. As students enter the workforce, graduates will be skilled at using the sponsors' latest tools and technology, and be more likely to use those tools and products on the job. Also, businesses can use the facility to train their employees or demo their products for potential customers. For example, the Graphics Department has an entrustment with Océ. The partnership has created a cutting edge, advanced technology learning center for graphic arts. Through this partnership the school received over a million dollars in equipment and technology and is the print shop for the entire City of Worcester. The Automotive Technology Department is called the Harr-Toyota Service Center due to the generous donation from Harr-Toyota. Their $100,000.00 donation has allowed us to create a 16 bay service center furnished and equipped with new state of the art automotive technology. This department services over 250 vehicles per month. Worcester Tech has also partnered with L'Oreal Redken to feature a full service beauty salon and day spa. The Worcester Credit Union was approached during the construction phase to provide a full service bank in the school. The Finance and Marketing students are employed, during the school day, to be the bank tellers. Since 2006, the bank has trained over 80 bank tellers for Central Massachusetts' needs.

Worcester Technical High School is committed to building partnerships with local two and four year colleges and universities. A successful example of these partnerships is the Tufts at Tech animal clinic that was created by a school partnership with Tufts University to provide affordable animal care for low-income families in the Worcester area. Tufts University funds a veterinarian to run the clinic and WTHS students work alongside providing animal care. The clinic services over 250 animals per month and charges 75% less than what a regular vet would charge. Teachers created authentic learning experiences in all facets of this partnership. The carpentry, plumbing, and electrical students built the veterinary clinic. The graphic students created the name and designed the logo and brochures and the painting and design students created the signage.

Community

Worcester Technical High School is committed to giving back to the community. Some examples include: at Green Hill Park, adjacent to our school, students have built the club house for the golf course with the Construction Academy, assisted in maintaining the barn yard zoo with the Veterinary Assisting Program, and provided land maintenance and water testing with the Environmental Tech Program. Students have refurbished several condemned multi-family homes within the city. They have also built a multi-family LEED certified house, from the ground up, for low-income Worcester residents. In addition, the students and staff designed and fabricated over 250 holiday wreaths that adorn downtown during the holiday season. This has brought great pride to our citizens and students alike.

STEM Focus

Two years ago, Worcester Technical High School became a STEM Career and College Innovation School. Innovation Schools are schools that operate with more autonomy and flexibility with staffing, professional development, policies and curriculum. Innovation Schools implement innovative strategies to improve student performance while maintaining their public school funding. Worcester Technical High School, under the Innovation School legislation, has a focus on STEM (Science, Technology, Engineering, and Math) education where students are taught an integrated curriculum which will help them to obtain STEM jobs upon graduation or study STEM related fields in college. With this 21st century focus, WTHS is training students to meet the employment demands of the area's growing biomedical, technology, and manufacturing industries. These partnerships will keep jobs in Worcester for another 100 years and keep our city/region strong and viable.

An example of a STEM project with higher education partnerships is the Solatrium, a modular, zero-energy home that competed in the US Department of Energy's Solar Decathlon which was held in Datong, China this past summer. Through working with post secondary linkages and area business/industry, the manufacturing and construction programs at WTHS partnered with one of 23 teams selected to compete in China. The collegiate team composed of engineering students from Worcester Polytechnic Institute, U.S.; Polytechnic Institute of New York University, U.S.; and Ghent University, Belgium, designed the home but needed assistance and expertise with the construction phase. WTHS instructors from plumbing, electrical, HVAC/R, machining, and welding stepped forward to lead their students in completing this state-of-the-art, green construction project on schedule. The modular home was built locally, tested, and then disassembled for shipment to China. Through the generosity of business/industry, six WTHS students and two instructors accompanied the team to China for reassembly and participated in the competition. Through the leadership efforts of the instructors at WTHS, inner-city students in an urban public school worked alongside elite engineering students to develop and hone their skills on the latest technologies in their respective trades and saw the fruit of their labor in a truly once-in-a-lifetime global cultural experience.

In addition, with the help and support of our local community college and business sector donations, WTHS's Robotics Team competed in local and regional competitions which qualified the team to compete in the Vex World Championship competition in Anaheim, California last April. The WTHS Vex Robotics Team competed against 426 teams representing 24 different countries and won the Vex Robotics World Championship.

Successful technical schools require strong links to the community, business and industry, and academic institutions. The school's success and the city's/region's success are intertwined.

WTHS is part of the economic engine, coordinating the needs and desires of industry for a highly-trained, adaptable workforce with the needs and desires of our students to secure good paying, rewarding jobs in the fields of their choice.

Background

Worcester Technical High School has been in existence since 1910. It is one of the first vocational schools built in the United States. Through the decades the facility became antiquated, the infrastructure incapable of being updated, and the equipment to train students was obsolete. In 1997, the New England Association of Schools and Colleges' Commission voted unanimously that the school be placed on probation for failure to meet the Commission's Standard 10 on School Facilities. In addition to an aging facility, Worcester Technical High School was the lowest performing high school in the city and one of the lowest performing vocational/technical schools in the state. In 2000, 97% of the students scored in the Needs Improvement and Failing Categories of the ELA MCAS exams, with 76% of these in the Failing Category. On the MCAS mathematics exams, 97% scored in the Needs Improvement and Failing Categories, with 85% of these students in the Failing Category. Students were not graduating career or college ready.

The business community, state and local officials, educational, and community leaders, and parents came together to support, fund, and design a new $90 million, state of the art vocational/technical facility. Worcester Technical High School is designed using the small learning community model. Funding from the Carnegie Foundation Planning Grant and a federally funded Small Learning Community Implementation Grant allowed our large high school of twenty-four technical programs to divide into four small learning communities (SLCs). This model provided a personalized learning community that supported all students, both academically and technically. It also fostered integrated academics, project based learning by incorporating real world applications, and engaging students in their learning to properly prepare them for career and college.

Awards

In 2006, School Planning and Management Magazine awarded our school the Impact on Learning Award in the category of non-traditional learning space. In 2009, WTHS was selected as one of 15 public high schools featured in How High Schools Become Exemplary by the Achievement Gap Initiative at Harvard University. In 2011, the National Association of Secondary School Principals (NASSP) selected WTHS as a MetLife Foundation-NASSP Breakthrough School. This national award is presented to five high schools and five middle schools across the country, and WTHS was the only high school selected in New England. The award recognizes schools achieving outstanding student gains in high poverty areas. I was one of two Breakthrough School award recipient principals (one middle and one high school) invited to present at a congressional briefing sponsored by the NASSP and the Alliance for Excellent Education Event at an event in May 2011. In 2012 and 2013, my school was selected as a Breaking Ranks Showcase School at the NASSP National Conferences. In 2013, I was selected as the Massachusetts Principal of the Year and as I already mentioned, just last week I was selected as the 2014 MetLife/NASSP National High School Principal of the Year.

The Role of the Principal

When I had the good fortune to be hired to open the new WTHS in 2004, I brought a unique combination of experience, knowledge, and skills with me. The success of our school is the result of many factors, and my contributions are squarely connected to my prior work and experience. The success of our school is the result of our redefining the role of vocational/technical education. In doing so, we have emphasized academic standards, teamwork, and motivation.

My background in a suburban high school prompted me to develop programs with extensive college preparatory experiences for students and to hold them accountable to high academic standards. The technical components of our vocational programs provided an opportunity to make rigorous programming relevant.

All important decisions at WTHS are made by the instructional leadership team, which includes me, the assistant principals, the vocational/technical director, and the department heads in the academic and technical areas. Our team works together to identify focused goals and targeted professional development and to develop a school culture that is marked by high expectations for teachers and students. Our team also makes every effort to coordinate professional development on the basis of intensive analysis of student data. Faculty members use that analysis to develop targeted interventions for students and respond to the high expectations of our school culture by becoming and remaining experts in their content fields.

NASSP and our members strongly support the Carl D. Perkins Career and Technical Education Act, which we feel has great potential to promote a personalized learning environment for each student through strong curriculum and instruction, and will increase student achievement through integrated academic and CTE programs. As we think about the law's reauthorization, we hope that the committee will stay focused on the program's ability to: 1) prepare all students for postsecondary education and work opportunities; 2) support and enhance academic achievement and technical literacy; and, 3) improve high schools to ensure higher student achievement and graduation for all students.

————

Chairman ROKITA. Mr. Fischer, you are recognized for 5 minutes.

STATEMENT OF JOHN FISCHER, DEPUTY COMMISSIONER, TRANSFORMATION & INNOVATION, VERMONT AGENCY OF EDUCATION

Mr. FISCHER. Chairman Rokita, Congressman Grijalva, and members of the subcommittee, thank you for inviting me here today. As deputy commissioner of education in Vermont I am responsible for our innovation and transformation agenda, with particular focus on career and technical education. And this year I also have the honor of serving as president of the National Association of State Directors of Career and Technical Education Consortium.

As you take up the important work of reauthorizing the Federal investment in CTE, I appreciate this opportunity to share insights based upon my experiences in Vermont, as well as those of my colleagues across the country. Let me start by saying the Federal investment in CTE is vitally important, and has been and continues to be a major driver of innovation. Twelve million students of all ages across the country participate in CTE programs in every type of community setting—urban, suburban and rural. And CTE programs are delivered at numerous types of educational settings at the secondary and post-secondary levels.

This diversity is a strength and a reflection of CTE's responsiveness to its community, employers, and students. It is also this diversity that makes the unity behind a common vision for the future of CTE so unique. In 2010 the State CTE directors from across the country agreed to a common vision for CTE, charting a progressive agenda that leverages opportunities presented in the Perkins legislation. This vision, which has been provided as a supplement to my testimony, seeks to break down the silos between academic and technical education and between secondary and post-secondary education. It calls for strengthened partnerships with employers and demands data-driven decision making. And it cements our commitment to a delivery system of programs of study organized around the national Career Clusters, which are 16 at this point. This vision guides our work, our Federal policy priorities, and my remarks today.

CTE is leading educational innovation and is at the nexus of economic and workforce development. BMW located in South Carolina because of the promise of its workforce, and CTE was an important part of that State's commitment to ensure that BMW has the skilled workforce that it needs today and tomorrow. In my State, as is the case in many across the country, CTE is helping to restore and grow our economy. CTE is updating existing programs like automotive, HVAC, advanced manufacturing, all of these to reflect the changing workplace and technologies, and introducing new programs like biomedical, computer science, mechatronics, culinology, nano-technology and the like to support emerging demands. These programs prepare students with adaptable skills and knowledge— exactly what employers want. CTE is serving a vital role in keeping States and the U.S. economy growing and innovating.

CTE's partnership with employers is one of the most treasured aspects of our history. From local mom-and-pop small businesses to industry giants like IBM, Marriott, Union Pacific, CMT, and Toyota, companies are investing in their future by building robust partnerships with education. From equipment donations to building curriculum, creating new schools, offering teachers and faculty externships, and providing students with internships, these business-education partnerships are essential to assuring our programs meet the needs of 21st century's economies.

Today's economy requires students to be prepared for options, which means being prepared for both post-secondary education and careers. CTE programs allow students to explore careers and be challenged by real world, authentic experiences. They get to apply their knowledge and skills, learn how to become members of teams, find focus, motivation, and confidence. Students are often learning and earning at the same time, gaining portable, industry and post-secondary credentials along the way.

Dual and concurrent enrollment has been a successful CTE policy in Vermont and across the country. Research has found that dual-enrollment students were more likely to earn a high school diploma, go on to college, persist at that level, and have a higher post-secondary grade point average than their peers. Not only do these opportunities give students a head start in post-secondary education, but lessens the college debt load. For example, at Ballard Memorial High School in Kentucky students in the health science program have the opportunity to graduate from high school and earn an associate degree. This is college and career readiness and this is today's CTE.

With Perkins funding and requirements as a national catalyst, CTE is transitioning its delivery model to programs of study, organized around the 16 Career Clusters. Driven by high-quality college and career ready standards, through the Common Career Technical Core, there is strong evidence that programs of study are producing positive outcomes, including better test results, better secondary GPAs, and improved progress toward graduation.

In my State, programs of study are playing a transformational role in ensuring that our most rural communities have access to high-quality CTE. In urban centers like New York, LA, Chicago, CTE is transforming high schools. This is a matter of equity. No matter your zip code, gender, socioeconomic status, or race, all students should have access to programs that prepare them to be both college and career ready.

And finally, none of this matters unless we have evidence of outcomes. In Vermont the graduation rate for CTE students is 93 percent compared to our overall graduation rate of 87 percent, and this is not unique to Vermont.

Chairman ROKITA. Thank you Mr. Fischer.

Mr. FISCHER. Thank you very much.

[The statement of Mr. Fischer follows:]

Prepared Statement of John Fischer, Deputy Commissioner, Transformation & Innovation, Vermont Agency of Education

Thank you for the opportunity to share my thoughts on Career Technical Education, or CTE. As the Deputy Commissioner of Education in Vermont, I am responsible for our innovation and transformation agenda, with particular focus on CTE, including standards, assessments, accountability, educator quality, school effectiveness, Federal programs, and public assurance of our State education system.

This year, I also have the honor of serving as the President of the National Association of State Directors of Career Technical Education Consortium. Established in 1920, the Consortium serves as the professional society of state and territory agency heads responsible for public CTE at the secondary, postsecondary, and adult levels in all fifty states, five U.S. territories, and the District of Columbia.

As you take up the important work of reauthorizing the federal investment in Career Technical Education, I appreciate the opportunity to share insights based not only upon my experiences in Vermont, but on those of my colleagues across the country. The federal investment in CTE is vitally important and has been, and continues to be, a major driver of change and innovation in CTE.

If I were to ask you "What is Career Technical Education?" many of you would have different answers. These responses would be driven by your own experiences and observations of CTE programs in your district. And none of your answers would be wrong. This is because CTE is diverse and responsive to the needs of the community, students and employers it serves.[1] CTE serves 12 million students of all ages—middle school through adults—across the country.[2] There are CTE programs in every state and in every type of community setting—urban, suburban and rural. And CTE programs are offered at myriad types of educational settings—comprehensive high schools, career academies, theme-based CTE high schools, community colleges, technical colleges, regional technical centers, and technical institutes. This diversity is a strength and a testament to the responsiveness of the CTE leadership and programs. But it is also this diversity that makes the unity behind a common vision for the future of CTE so unique and compelling.

High-Quality CTE: Preparing Students for Jobs of the Future

In 2010, in recognition of the changing economic forces, and to further advance the CTE field, State CTE Directors agreed upon a common vision for CTE. This vision was informed by key stakeholder groups in industry, the broader education community, and government representatives. The vision, agreed to by all the states, charted a progressive agenda that leveraged the opportunities presented by the federal legislation. The vision honors the rich history of vocational education. It holds us accountable for the ongoing transformation of programs to be responsive to the needs of the economy. And it charts a bold and progressive course for the future that seeks to break down the silos between academic and technical education, and between secondary and postsecondary education. It calls for employers to be co-developers, co-owners of CTE programs. It demands data-driven decision-making. And it cements our commitment to a delivery system organized by the 16 Career Clusters(r) and delivered through comprehensive programs of study.

This vision guides our federal policy priorities and our actions, and is comprised for five inter-connected principles:

Principle 1: CTE is critical to ensuring that the United States leads in global competitiveness.

Education is critical to ensure the global competitiveness of the United States, and some stakeholders and policymakers even consider it an issue of national security. State CTE Directors recognize the importance of delivering CTE programs that meet the needs of the labor market and the global economy and, thus, drive the nation's ability to compete globally.

How is CTE responding to the global economy? In the southeastern part of the United States, CTE is part of state economic development strategies. States like South Carolina, which worked with BMW to build their U.S. operations in Greenville/Spartanburg. Or Alabama, which is home to a Toyota plant. Oklahoma brought in the aerospace industry. Louisville, Kentucky, has GE. And right outside the beltway, Virginia won the bid for VW. These companies are locating to these states because of their workforce—and CTE plays an important part of ensuring that current and future workers are prepared for careers in that regional economy.

Also, CTE is introducing new programs to meet the needs of the modern economy like mechatronics, culinology, biotechnology, nano-technology, green energy, etc. Today's CTE students are prepared with adaptable skills and knowledge for the ever-changing economy. These students have focus. They have drive. They have expertise. They have work experience, in large part due to their participation in the Career Technical Student Organizations. They have what employers want. At a time when employers complain that graduates are not prepared to fill job vacancies, CTE is delivering. If you attend national Career Technical Student Organization competitions like SkillsUSA, which was held in Louisville this summer, you'll see students walk away with not only a medal of recognition for their performance in a particular competitive event focused on technical skills, but also multiple job offers which often include support for continued education.

Another example of this innovation and responsiveness to the needs of the economy and the demand of the modern learner is the Vermont Virtual AcademySM. The virtual academy provides an alternative to the traditional in-classroom k-12 experience and instead allows students to learn at their own pace in an environment of their choosing through their computer and an Internet connection. Increasingly, online schools such as Vermont's Virtual Academy have helped to improve student performance and achievement through a more flexible and modern delivery system. This blended learning approach lends itself well to Vermont's priority Career Clusters, Information Technologies and STEM. This dynamic and innovative educational programs seeks to fulfill the constantly evolving needs of every student.

I recently heard about a student who was able to take part in this program. Kevin, a student at Spaulding High School in Vermont, is involved in a number of team sports for his school along with a leadership position on the student council. He is also a budding entrepreneur and recently opened his own lawn care business. Ultimately, he would like to go on to college and become an Engineer. According to Kevin, "The things I read and learn in my class each day, make me feel more confident in what I plan on doing after college." The CTE programs and blended learning opportunities such as our Virtual Learning Academy offered through Vermont's Virtual Learning Cooperative have helped clearly Kevin realize his full potential.

Principle 2: CTE actively partners with employers to design and provide high-quality, dynamic programs.

CTE's partnership with employers is one of the most treasured aspects of our history and continues to be at the heart of our programs today. Our vision statement calls for an even stronger partnership with employers by having business and industry having an increased role in the design and delivery of CTE programs of study.

Across the nation, CTE leaders are collaborating with business and industry. For example, Union Pacific Railroad works with local schools through their Direction Recruitment Education and Mentoring (DREAM) program in which employees provide students with career, educational and social guidance. The mentoring program serves as a vehicle to develop students' self-esteem and confidence in their personal and career ambitions as they explore the business world.

Partnerships with employers provide students with real-world and real-work problems to solve. They provide teachers and faculty with externships and students with internships, work-based learning experiences and mentorship. These experiences are essential for students to test the waters and gain early exposure to a variety of career fields. This exploration of what students like to do and are good at can help them find focus and confidence—which leads to higher aspirations. We see this over and over.

We believe federal CTE legislation can help promote improved employer-education engagement and partnerships, including requiring local advisory committees comprised of employers and education stakeholders to actively partner in the design and delivery CTE high-quality programs of study. Further, comprehensive career guidance and development programs and personalized learning plans beginning in middle school are essential to helping expand access to CTE and ensuring more students have the support they need to learn about careers, explore options, understand the necessary course of study and experiences essential to be successful in their college and career journey.

Principle 3: CTE prepares students to succeed in further education and careers.

As described earlier, CTE has evolved considerably over the last decade. High-quality CTE programs prepare students to be successful by providing adaptable skills and knowledge, thereby ensuring flexibility to transition careers as interests change, opportunities emerge, technology advances, and the economy transforms. It is no longer acceptable or appropriate to talk about college or careers. It must be college and careers.[3]

This transformation in expectation from ''or'' to ''and'' is underscored by the data. Researchers project that, by 2020, 35% of jobs will require at least a bachelor's degree and 30% will require some postsecondary education.[4] Focusing on preparing secondary CTE students for postsecondary education is paying off; the college attendance rate for CTE students increased by nearly 32% between 1982 and 1992, and the trend continues.[5] Even so, more work needs to be done. Only 70% of high school graduates study at a postsecondary institution immediately after high school, and far fewer complete a degree or credential.[6] Improving transitions between secondary and postsecondary education is one of the most efficient ways to lead students to postsecondary success. Thus, the focus of the federal investment on preparation for both college and careers and the linkages between the learner levels is absolutely necessary.

One way CTE has been successful at promoting learner level alignment is through decades of work around dual and concurrent enrollment. A recent Community College Research Center study found that dual enrollment students in Florida were more likely to earn a high school diploma, go on to college, persist at that level for longer, and have a higher postsecondary grade point average than their peers.[7]

In recent years, efforts in states like Alabama, Colorado, Georgia, Ohio, West Virginia and Pennsylvania have expanded toward statewide initiatives to promote acquisition and portability of postsecondary credits while students are still in high school. In addition, we have seen the expansion of the inclusion of Advanced Placement courses in CTE programs of study. And there are some programs out there that really have taken this to a whole new level. Ballard Memorial High School in Ballard County, Kentucky provides students in the school's Health Science program the opportunity to graduate high school and earn an associate's degree from Western Kentucky Community & Technical College at the same time.

These opportunities give students a head start on college and lessen the economic burden of attending postsecondary institutions. Employers, too, benefit from these partnerships as they are able to confidently hire qualified individuals to fill job vacancies.

The quality of CTE educators cannot be overlooked as a major component to student success. In Vermont, state leaders have developed an innovative CTE teacher professional development program that will start in the 2013-2014 school year. Vermont will now not only have one of the best licensing programs for CTE teachers initially licensed to teach, but will now also have a seamless pathway to earning a Bachelor's degree in Career and Technical Education in a 3+2 program in partnership with the state college system. As the economy evolves and the needs of the labor market change, CTE students are uniquely positioned to thrive in a globally-competitive environment with the skills and knowledge base first acquired through rigorous CTE programs taught by knowledgeable, prepared CTE instructors.

Principle 4: CTE is delivered through comprehensive programs of study aligned to the National Career Clusters Framework.

States have largely embraced the National Career Clusters(r) Framework, which includes 16 Career Clusters and 79 Career Pathways, as the organizer for modern CTE. With Perkins funding and requirements as the national catalyst, CTE is transitioning its delivery model of CTE programs to programs of study. What's different about programs of study?

Programs of study are designed to seamlessly link a student's secondary and postsecondary education through a structured sequence of academic and CTE courses that leads to a postsecondary-level credential. In a program of study, the standards, curriculum, and assessments are aligned, thereby ensuring coordination and seamless delivery of instruction and transitions for students. Relevant work-based learning opportunities, Career Technical Student Organizations, comprehensive career planning, and leadership development are offered. And there is evidence that programs of study are producing positive outcomes. A study conducted through the National Research Center for Career and Technical Education last year found that students who were enrolled in a program of study had better test scores, better secondary GPAs, and made more progress towards graduation than their peers.[8]

In addition, states have been working to add clarity and rigor to academic and technical instruction at the high school level, with the goal of better preparing students for college and careers and, thus, improving the nation's ability to be globally competitive. Perkins requires CTE programs to be aligned to rigorous, state-adopted academic and CTE standards that define what students should know and be able to do after completing instruction in a program of study. To that end, CTE has been an advocate for college and career-ready standards. Last year, State CTE Directors from 42 states, the District of Columbia and Palau, embraced the opportunity to improve CTE through high-quality, voluntary CTE standards, organized by Career Cluster, that define what students should know and be able to do after completing instruction in a program of study.

Programs of study also promote coordination and collaboration between secondary and postsecondary partners. Consortia efforts that protect funding streams but promote statewide collaboration have proven vital to improving the capacity and scalability of CTE programs of study. Consortia can provide a unified state effort towards comparable quality of educational and training programming across all subsets of the population. They also ensure equitable geographic access for students, spanning middle school through high school, apprenticeships and college, as well as lifelong learning. Additionally, consortia help develop performance assessments of a valid and reliable nature to further improve the state's accountability system., help define new competency models and strategies to strengthen the link between CTE programs and the needs of the labor market and the economy.

Principle 5: CTE is a results-driven system that demonstrates a positive return on investment.

Finally, CTE embraces the critical importance of accountability and data-driven decisions. Data have consistently illustrated CTE's positive return on investment. The fiscal impact of a reduced drop-out rate, cost savings for employers, and other positive impacts on regional, state, and national economies show how investment in CTE results in positive economic gains on the whole. Wisconsin's technical colleges return a public benefit of $10.65 for every dollar invested, and taxpayers in Los Angeles County see a 10 percent return on their investment in the county's community colleges.[9] These are just a few of the many examples where CTE is yielding positive economic results across the country.

In Washington's Workforce Training and Education Coordinating Board commissioned one of the most compelling studies on the return on investment for CTE. Composed of nine representatives from business, labor, and government, the board found that CTE students in Washington earn more on average, and thus pay back the state's investment in their education through increased tax revenue. Ultimately, the return on investment for CTE students in Washington was an impressive seven times the original public investment.[10]

Unfortunately, the sort of data Washington is able to compile is not available to every state due to limitations of their data systems. There is a need to create common definitions across the states, common performance measures across similar federal education and workforce programs and to increase alignment across K-12 education, postsecondary education and workforce data systems.

Conclusion

In 2006, the language in the Perkins Act was updated from "vocational and technical education" to "career and technical education." This transition was more than just a name change. It represented a fundamental shift in philosophy from CTE being for those who were not going to college to a system that prepares students for both employment and postsecondary education. CTE leaders embraced the goals of Perkins IV. We strengthened the integration of high-quality academic and technical education programs, further emphasizing that students participating in CTE must meet the same rigorous academic standards as all other students. Many states went beyond the law's minimal program of study requirements. We made great progress in improving our data systems. And as a result, CTE students have succeeded. The national average graduation rate for CTE students is over 90 percent, while the average national graduation rate for all students is less than 74 percent.[11] CTE students are out-performing academic benchmarks:

CTE indicator	Target performance	Actual performance
Reading/Language Arts (Secondary)	67%	72%
Mathematics (Secondary)	59%	63%
Technical Skill Attainment (Secondary)	68%	75%

CTE indicator	Target performance	Actual performance
Technical Skill Attainment (Postsecondary)	70%	82%

And 70 percent of CTE concentrators stayed in postsecondary education or transferred to a 4-year degree program (compared to the overall average state target of 58%) and transitioned to postsecondary education or employment by December of the year of graduation.[12]

Career Technical Education is learning that works for America. My colleagues and I from across the nation believe that in that the federal investment is vital to ensuring that we achieve the vision we put forth in 2010—ensuring that all students have access to high-quality CTE programs. As we look to the future, imagine an education and workforce system that rewards innovation, cohesively supports different learning styles, equally values different interests and talents, nimbly adapts and responds to technology and workplace needs, and prepares all students for career success through multiple pathways. Our nation's economic vitality hinges on our commitment to invest in and ensure the preparedness, efficiency, innovation, creativity and productivity of the U.S. workforce, and CTE is instrumental to our success.

ENDNOTES

[1] U.S. Department of Education, Office of Planning, Evaluation and Policy Development. National Assessment of Career and Technical Education: Interim Report, 2013. Of note, The share of public high school graduates who are CTE investors, earning 3 or more occupational credits, was 38% in 2004. The share of CTE explorers, who earn three or more CTE occupational credits in more than one occupational area, increased to 21% in 2004.

[2] U.S. Department of Education, Office of Vocational and Adult Education. Carl D. Perkins Career and Technical Education Act Consolidated Annual Reports, 2011-2012.

[3] Career Readiness Partners Council's Career Readiness Definition: *http://www.careerreadynow.org/*

[4] Carnevale, Anthony, Nicole Smith, and Jeff Strohl, "Recovery: Job Growth and Education Requirements Through 2020," Georgetown University Center on Education and the Workforce, June 2013.

[5] U.S. Department of Education, Office of the Under Secretary, Policy and Program Studies Service, "National Assessment of Vocational Education: Final Report to Congress," Washington, D.C., 2004.

[6] National Science Foundation, "Science and Engineering Indicators 2012," Arlington, VA, 2012, *http://www.nsf.gov/statistics/seind12/c1/c1s4.htm*.

[7] Karp, Melinda Mechur, Juan Carlos Calcagno, Katherine L. Hughes, Dong Wook Jeong, & Thomas Bailey, "Dual Enrollment Students in Florida and New York City: Postsecondary Outcomes," Community College Research Center 37, February (2008): *http://ccrc.tc.columbia.edu/media/k2/attachments/dual-enrollment-student-outcomes-brief.pdf.*

[8] Castellano, M., Sundell, K., Overman, L. T., & Aliaga, O. A., "Do Career and Technical Education Programs of study Improve Student Achievement? Preliminary Analyses From a rigorous Longitudinal Study," International Journal of Educational Reform, 21 (2012): 98-118.

[9] Association for Career and Technical Education, "Investing in Career & Technical Education Yields Big Returns."

[10] "CTE: An Investment in Success," Workforce Training and Education Coordinating Board, Olympia, Washington, *http://www.wtb.wa.gov/Documents/CTESuccess.pdf.*

[11] U.S. Department of Education, Office of Vocational and Adult Education, "Carl D. Perkins Career and Technical Education Act of 2006, Report to Congress on State Performance, Program Year 2007—08," Washington, D.C., 2010.

[12] U.S. Department of Education, "FY 2010 Annual Performance Report," Washington, D.C., 2011. *http://www2.ed.gov/about/reports/annual/2010report/fy2010-apr.pdf.*

––––––––––

Chairman ROKITA. Mr. Britt, you are now recognized for 5 minutes.

STATEMENT OF FRANK BRITT, CHIEF EXECUTIVE OFFICER, PENN FOSTER INC.

Mr. BRITT. Thank you very much and good morning, Chairman Rokita and Congressman Grijalva and the esteemed members of this committee. My name is Frank Britt and I am the CEO of Penn Foster, one of the Nation's largest and most experienced providers of online and hybrid education in the career technical field. I appreciate the opportunity to share some perspectives this morning regarding this vital part of the education economy.

I come to you today as a practitioner, as an active observer of CTE, and my perspective starts with several important assumptions. The first is that it is self-evident that CTE has worked and has improved the lives of millions of people due to dedicated faculty and administrators and strong State and Federal policies. Secondly, given that strong track record, there is a lot that has worked and a lot should be embraced going forward. This is not a part of the education economy that is broken, it is one that is thriving and can continue to improve for the future. Thirdly, change is upon us. Society is changing, education itself is changing, employers' expectations of workers are changing, and the reality is the learning habits of students is evolving in a digital world.

It is in this context that I think there is a significant opportunity to build on the strong and vital role of CTE, the one that it already plays today in schools and in business across our country. I think we need to continue to lay out a road map and a platform for CTE that will further establish it in a contemporary context. That road map should be formulated by seasoned practitioners in the CTE industry as well as administrators, but it also needs to include people from outside the CTE industry to help shape the next generation of students and lifelong learners.

As you have read in my submitted remarks, we have six recommendations, and I wanted to highlight just three of those. But what they share in common—and this is an important point—is all of them have been implemented in other parts of the education economy and in other sectors of the corporate economy, and that is an important point to note. Our objective is to encourage the melding of proven best practices in CTE with the best practices and insights we have gained from other industries so we can optimize the student experience of CTE, as well as the return on investment.

We have three recommendations particularly we thought worth noting. The first is diffuse project-based learning with the best of traditional practices to better personalize the student experience. This means project-based learning combined with the way traditional ground-based academics work to drive the best outcome for the students.

Number two, we want to embrace digital learning. CTE faculty members have always needed to embrace new technologies given the disciplines they teach. Given that technology and software are essential to countless vocational fields already, we see embedding further digital tools in the learning context as a natural extension of what happens in the classroom and what should happen out of the classroom going forward.

The third is a change in perception. The reality is that the middle-skills occupations are in fact in demand, extraordinarily respectable occupations, and drive stable lifestyles. In many cases it allows people to advance to middle management, even senior management positions. But as we also know, the degrees that prepare students for middle-skill careers are often misunderstood and underappreciated. The reality is that the alternative education career pathway is in fact compelling for millions of capable traditional learners and adults, and it needs to be encouraged by people and organizations of influence.

There is a significant opportunity to make CTE a new way to think about the economy for millions of people, and we think the perception and branding of CTE needs to be evolved. It needs to become a mainstream solution that is embraced in the same way that traditional 4-year colleges are embraced. We all know that a 4-year degree may not be desirable or even practical for every student, or in some cases it maybe shouldn't be the first step. The reality of that is the trillion dollars in student loan debt.

Our assertion is that students and adults alike should be encouraged to understand this vibrant set of career alternatives to help themselves and their families build a more productive life. This is a moment to lean in on affirming the power and the promise of CTE-enabled careers.

In summary, we are supporters of CTE, we know it can play a vital role in helping address the acute skills gap in this country, which is likely to worsen with the resurgence of U.S. manufacturing. We have a 123-year history at our organization, including our 100,000 students today who participate in all aspects of our high school, our college, as well as our vocational programs and career programs. There is an imperative and an opportunity to change CTE in this country, and we think it is an exciting one that can improves everyone's lives. We appreciate the opportunity to share our perspectives on that subject.

Chairman ROKITA. Thank you, Mr. Britt.

[The statement of Mr. Britt follows:]

Prepared Statement of Frank F. Britt, CEO, Penn Foster

Good Morning, Chairman Rokita, Congressman Grijalva, and esteemed members of the committee, my name is Frank Britt. I am the CEO of Penn Foster—a leader in career-focused online and hybrid education with a commitment to addressing the middle skills gap in America.

The story of Penn Foster is rooted in training Americans with the technical skills needed to find jobs where they live. In 1869, in one of the largest mining disasters in the history of Pennsylvania, a massive fire caused the death of 110 workers, due in large part to a lack of training and expertise among the miners. This crippled the coal mines in the area and left people out of work and under-skilled. In response, newspaper editor Thomas Foster founded the International Correspondence School in 1890, to train miners on engineering and safety. Foster pioneered correspondence learning because his students did not have the means to travel every day to sit in a classroom. As the school reached its one millionth enrollment Thomas Edison, who authored one of its courses, remarked that home study was one of the greatest inventions of the 20th century. President Theodore Roosevelt agreed. He visited the Scranton campus and extolled the virtues of the school's study method. Soon Foster's programs grew and became more sophisticated, and the International Correspondence School became Penn Foster. In the years since, our institution has produced many notable alumni including Chrysler's former president Walter Chrysler, GM's former president Charles W. Nash and Dan Kimball, former Secretary of the U.S. Navy.

Since our inception, more than 13 million people have enrolled in Penn Foster, which encompasses a high school, career school, and college. Today, Penn Foster enrolls approximately 150,000 students annually in programs consistent with traditional schools and community colleges, providing fully accredited high school diplomas, career programs and certificates, and bachelor's and associate degrees. Our Career School, College, and High School have all met the high standards of academic integrity set by the Accrediting Commission of the Distance Education and Training Council (DETC), a nationally recognized accrediting agency, and various other accreditation bureaus including regionally accreditation for Penn Foster High School and Career School by the Commission on Secondary Schools of the Middle States Association of Colleges and Schools.

We focus on traditional age high school students through adult learners and partner with over 400 secondary and post-secondary institutions that use Penn Foster content and delivery platforms to expand their offerings. For example, Polk County School District in Florida uses Penn Foster's curriculum and platform to re-attract students who have dropped out of high school and help them graduate. We also attack the systematic issues of the drop-out crisis by contributing senior leadership and resources to the National Dropout Prevention Network, which has worked to create opportunities for all young people to fully develop academic, social, work, and life skills.

Given that our students are often balancing full-time jobs and/or other familial responsibilities, Penn Foster has become an industry leader in crafting innovative solutions to keep them on-track. We employ a self-paced educational model based on subject matter mastery that allows our students to set their own timetables without falling behind while accounting for personal circumstances.

Our student-centered approach extends to program cost and payment options. We make sure that our programs do not require students to take on excessive debt obligations. For example, the average starting salary for a Pharmacy Technician is $28,400. Penn Foster's Pharmacy Tech certificate program cost students less than $500 (over 60% less than most alternatives). For school districts using Penn Foster career electives and high school courses this means low cost options that fit within the school's budget and allow them to sponsor innovative models for educating their high school population.

In addition, for individual consumers or students, paying for school is more manageable under our pay-as-you-go model. We do not accept federal student aid programs under Title IV of the Higher Education Amendments including Stafford Student and the Federal Pell Grant Program. Instead, monthly payments are calibrated to match academic progress and students' ability to pay, which better aligns objectives between students and the institution including our high school, career and college. For example, the cost of our associate and bachelor's degrees are about 30% less than community colleges and 70% less than traditional four year institutions.

For many, our programs are a gateway to the respectable salary and stable lifestyle that accompany careers in vocations traditionally classified as "middle-skilled." For others, we smooth the transition to higher education by simplifying the credit transfer process. This is nothing less than the democratization of education, as we offer our students access to the best in technology, community and academics, as well as a support system usually reserved for those who can afford high tuition and the accompanying loan payments. And by harnessing the benefits of scale economies, we are able to do so at a lower cost.

Given our position as one of the nation's largest and most experienced providers of online instruction in Career Technical Education (CTE) at the high school and post-secondary level, we appreciate the opportunity to address the Subcommittee and offer recommendations to improve the funding, delivery, and promotion of CTE.

Recommendations to Make CTE More Efficient and Effective

To date, a lot of good has been done. Lives have been changed and skills have been built, as institutions and dedicated faculty have been well-preparing students for careers in CTE. We are here today to talk about how to build on the strong foundation of CTE and evolve the system while innovating for the future. We have six recommendations to improve career and technical education in our country today:

1. Employ project based learning to personalize the student experience
2. Embrace digital learning
3. Change the perception
4. Stimulate innovation
5. Promote data uniformity
6. Reward competency, not accreditation

We recognize the Subcommittee and Staff have deep expertise in a variety of issues related to CTE and the Perkins Act, and will direct our remarks to areas that may complement this panel's deep experiences. The basis of these viewpoints is as a practitioner, rather than a policy expert. We exist to provide education either directly to the learners, or support school districts, higher ed institutions and employers who seek alternative CTE delivery models. We share these perspectives based on directly interfacing with thousands of students each year, and as active observers of the incumbent delivery approaches and providers. Like many other organizations, we are seeking to navigate the new needs of the next generation CTE students, and be productive advocates and supporters of current faculty and administration and collaborate with them to better address the needs of both traditional and adult learners.

1. Employ project based learning to personalize the student experience

Project-based learning (PBL) is an educational approach that focuses on real-life application of theories and lessons and is in practice in many leading CTE schools across the country. Students engaged in PBL pursue solutions to nontrivial problems by asking and refining questions, debating ideas, making predictions, designing plans and experiments, collecting and analyzing data, drawing conclusions, and communicating their ideas and findings to others. This provides an alternative to paper-based, rote memorization, teacher-led classrooms. Proponents of project-based learning cite numerous benefits to the implementation of these strategies in the classroom including a greater depth of understanding of concepts, broader knowledge base, improved communication and interpersonal/social skills, enhanced leadership skills, increased creativity, and improved writing skills.

At present, the vast majority of funding is devoted to traditional infrastructure and practices. Instead, investments should be made to "mainstream" PBL enabled by online and hybrid courses that are personalized to directly benefit students. In these student-centered models the role of faculty often evolves. Instead of spending all of their time reviewing material, they are focused on the application of the material and tailoring that teaching to the individual needs of the learner.

2. Embrace digital learning

Much has changed since the Perkins Act was made law seven years ago, as more and more students are turning to custom CTE programs online.[1] Yet, the Act does not recognize online or hybrid models under its definition of "institution." Meanwhile, in the private sector, the service Khan Academy, a non-profit educational website whose mission is to provide "a free world-class education for anyone anywhere," educates millions each day with little-to-no overhead. With 260 million lessons and a staff of fewer than 100, Khan's results have been astounding. The innovation in their equation is simply the Internet itself, as noted by many leading experts, including Michael Staton, co-founder of Inigral.

The Committee should continue to encourage use of the Internet and digital learning in education at every opportunity, especially to perpetuate peer-to-peer platforms and social media enablement. These adaptive learning engines will contain intelligent programs that understand and respond to each student's level of competency.

For example, tech-enabled and hybrid educational delivery platforms can optimize total spending per student by using predictive tools that automate intervention and augment student-progress, while increasing faculty productivity and moving from hard copy text to digital content. The goal is to deliver a student experience that drives academic progress and has built-in tools to catch students before they struggle. This includes using personalized and adaptive learning systems for teachers. These systems are complemented by greater parental, business, and community engagement and work through partnerships with local employers. The results would be higher attendance rates, higher effectiveness as measured by staying in school, progression, and most importantly more career and college pathways.

3. Change the perception

We recommend the public and private CTE institutions, together with the government, proactively educate the public on the value of careers in CTE fields. We have to be even more effective at communicating the narrative of why students and citizens should be compelled to embrace these careers. Explaining this story has always been essential, and now faces more complex marketing challenges as new social tools are introduced and mobile consumption becomes more prevalent. This will require new types of content, such as user generated reviews. To compete in that environment, CTE needs a national "Got Job?"-style campaign, funded by the private sector, to reach its target audiences (including students and parents) and penetrate the national consciousness. Led by a cross-section of leading employers and/or industry organizations, this campaign needs to involve Committee members and others in positions of influence and esteem to highlight CTE fields as providing rigorous, challenging curricula that lead to college and career readiness. Americans need to see "alternative pathways" not as code words for less potential and low wages, but instead as a viable, creditable and highly pragmatic academic and career roadmap for a significant number of traditional and adult students.

Historically CTE has suffered from negative perception, and flipping that perception may be the number one issue holding us back from filling these important jobs with skilled labor, and tackling the national jobs crisis.

4. Stimulate innovation

Career technical education is a $30 billion industry and impacts millions of learners each year, yet it has been largely ignored by entrepreneurs, venture capital and top executives from leading companies. Innovation is the key force that shapes industries, and more talented leaders need to be attracted to the sector to help conceive approaches and take advantage of emerging practices from the new education economy. While there are highly successful and innovative schools, such as Gateway Technical College, their influence is constrained by geography. To attract large-scale innovators and new sources of capital to drive research and development the delivery model and economic and regulatory environments will need to change.

CTE needs Perkins dollars directly focused on innovation grants, prizes and university collaboration to incentivize engagement and diversify the base of potential innovators.[2] Furthermore, new parties, including proprietary schools, need to have a say in the updated version of the Perkins Act and the national CTE agenda. Online and hybrid learning models can offer more affordable career and technical education for students while also reducing labor and operational costs for schools. As a result of these savings, more funding can be freed up to directly benefit students.[3]

This next-generation, technology-enabled career and technical education would simplify administrative and logistical tasks, leading to higher student and teacher satisfaction. For ground-based career tech schools partnering with the next generation providers can expand the radius of their coverage geographically, allow for new programs not offered today yet in demand locally, and also provide on-going continuing education to graduates. This will be of particular benefit to rural America where travel and class-size often constrain the ability of districts to offer CTE courses. Partnering with online CTE providers will ensure that rural students have the same access to high-demand CTE professions as their urban and suburban counterparts.

5. Promote data uniformity

Despite significant spending on CTE across the High School, Technical College and Career School sectors, the quality of unit-level and aggregate data on spending and student achievement is often elusive, contradictory, or out-of-date. For example, the basic definition of who and what is a K-12 CTE student varies across states and districts. Is a CTE student a "CTE concentrator" who takes 4-6 CTE courses in one area, or is it any student who takes any CTE course? The definition of what constitutes a CTE course varies across states, districts and even schools. A world-class educational system cannot be modernized without better data and consistency for the sake of benchmarking and performance improvement management on behalf of students and investors. Similarly, inconsistencies in how and who provides tracking and reporting costs impact how a given state's delivery system is set up: e.g., New York has a regional service center model (BOCES) that delivers some (but not all) CTE programs for its member school districts. Other states deliver CTE programs in comprehensive high schools. Those variables impact administrative, transportation, instructional, and capital costs.

Simplifying and unifying definitions and practices will save providers operating in multiple states time, money, and frustration, and will ultimately benefit students.

6. Reward competency, not accreditation

Education is entering a transitional moment. Moving forward we should embrace the best of the traditional model while incorporating the advantages of a competency-based system. The need to assure the public that an institution meets standards and delivers on its promises will remain essential, but the future is a movement toward competency-based education and away from credit-hour measures.

One option is for CTE (over time) to embrace an employer-driven competency-attainment based system to complement credit hours.[4] This will likely require panels of employers to set criteria for competencies needed to meet industry standards and regulation at the national level, which would eliminate, standardize or simplify state-by-state restrictions and barriers. An early example of these principles in action includes The National Coalition of Certification Centers (NC3), which were established to implement and sustain industry-recognized portable certifications with strong validation and assessment standards. As CTE makes the transition to competency-based certification, the online education will be uniquely positioned to serve learners in a variety of fields including Vet Tech and Pharma Tech, where competency programs are already operational.

Career Technical Education (CTE) at the High School Level

More than 850,000 K-12 students in the U.S. are classified as "vocational," which encompasses CTE fields and makes up just 2% of total students. The cost to educate these students is nearly $14,000 or 20-40% greater than that of traditional academic instruction. In recent years approximately $13 billion has been spent annually by federal, state and local governments to support youth-focused vocational education systems across the U.S., with federal funding constituting only about 4-8% percent of all state and local spending.[5] This is in addition to the $16 billion post-high school trade and technical school-industry.

Penn Foster is striving to make career technical education more affordable by combining online instruction with practical hands-on training. Unlike many CTE alternatives, including both traditional and online options, Penn Foster is fixated on our students' long-term goals. This allows us to eliminate any instruction that is not central to our students achieving in their desired fields, reducing student's tuition with no degradation of value. We take the same approach in our work with corporate partners, for whom we provide low-cost employee training programs online in a targeted and personalized manner.

A Commitment to Career Training: Penn Foster and Job Corps

Penn Foster's collaboration with Job Corps is just one example of our commitment to education innovation in career technical training with students who have struggled in the traditional system. Both Penn Foster and Job Corps are focused on bringing professional and educational opportunities to at-risk students and those who have not had success in the traditional system. Penn Foster operates in 50 of Job Corps' 125 centers around the nation, implementing our self-paced high school model and devising various innovative hybrid courses that combine online instruction with hands-on training. Since 2006, the partnership has worked by combining general high school requirements such as math or science with electives in a career track of the student's choice. Run simultaneously, Penn Foster provides the materials to help the students receive their diploma, while Job Corps provides them with the practical career training and support. An instructor is present at all times and helps the student decide on and prepare for their next exciting step, whether it's a job or college. When they complete the program students leave with more than just a diploma, they have a skill set that can help lead to a better life.

New Students and Career Paths

Higher education is increasingly seen as a requisite in today's job market. Yet there are profoundly troubling signs that the U.S. is failing to meet its obligation to prepare millions of young adults. In an era in which education has never been more important to economic success, the U.S. has fallen behind many other nations in educational attainment and achievement. Within the U.S. economy, there is also growing evidence of a "skills gap" in which many young adults lack the skills needed for many jobs that pay a middle-class wage. Simultaneously, there has been a dramatic decline in the ability of adolescents and young adults to find work. Indeed, the percentage of teens and young adults who have jobs is now at the lowest level since World War II.

As a result, the demographics of the "typical student" have changed and college students are no longer just 18-to-22-year-olds. They may be single working mothers in their 40s or grandparents in their 60s. They may seek traditional degrees or be part of the fastest growing career track—those pursuing career certificates. Significantly, the National Center for Education Statistics notes that 36% of today's college students are over age 25, a group that is expected to grow by 20 percent between 2010 and 2020.[6] As norms of age and income become obsolete, there is a need for more customization and flexibility in delivery methods to meet the needs of non-traditional students.

Just as students' backgrounds have changed, so have their career paths. Today, a person's first job no longer becomes a lifelong career, and students need to be more versatile than in previous generations. According to leading experts, between 60 and 70% of the jobs required 20 years from now do not exist today, a dramatic-yet-intuitive statistic given the countless number today's new careers that have only emerged over the past decade including in social media, green energy sustainability, cloud computing, and data science.

According to the Center on Education and the Workforce at Georgetown University, the U.S. economy will create some 47 million job openings over the 10-year period ending in 2018. Nearly two-thirds of these jobs will require at least some post-secondary education. Therefore, applicants without post-high school education will fill 36 percent of the job openings, or just half the percentage of jobs they held in the early 1970s. Moreover, the Center projects that 14 million openings will be filled by people with an associate's degree or occupational certificate. Many of those will be in "middle-skill" occupations such as electrician, construction manager, dental hygienist, paralegal and police officer. These jobs often have higher salaries than jobs held by those with bachelors' degrees. In fact, 27 percent of people with post-secondary licenses or certificates—credentials short of an associate's degree—earn more than the average bachelor's degree recipient. There will also be a huge number of job openings in so-called blue-collar fields like construction, manufacturing, and natural resources, which will provide nearly 8 million openings, an estimated 2.7 of which will require a post-secondary credential.

Given the dynamic nature of the marketplace, it is more important than ever for educators to provide employment-focused education. As students look to train-up and acquire practical and marketable skills, educators must respond in kind by adjusting their methods to be more learner-focused. Ideally, the future of education will blend online and traditional learning experiences and be flexible, so that the material is available to the student on his/her own time and teaching and engagement is saved for the classroom.

Penn Foster has helped answer the call with more than 200 partnerships with secondary and post-secondary schools and 35 state workforce development boards. We're making content available and allowing students to learn at their own paces, while providing in-person support and guidance to improve graduation rates.

Filling the Middle Skill Jobs of Today and Tomorrow

For many Americans, "higher education" still means a four-year degree. However, with unemployment hovering around 7.5 percent and with many students graduating from four-year institutions unable to find jobs, our perception of the costs and benefits of education needs to change. Degrees that prepare students for middle-skilled careers are often ignored or rejected, but education leaders need to realize that, as valuable as four-year degrees may be, they are not practical for every student, especially given that these students are saddled with an average of $26,600 of debt overall,[7] and $32,700 when graduating from for-profit colleges.[8] Instead of ignoring middle-skilled careers, we need to embrace them as viable alternatives to traditional degrees that lead to high-demand careers, and ensure that associated education costs remain affordable and aligned with salary potential.

Jobs traditionally known as "middle-skilled" will make up nearly half of all openings in the next 10 years,[9] and yet there is a lack of infrastructure, support, and data to help middle-skill workers navigate the market to discover and attain these jobs. As a result, too many middle-skill workers are enrolling in four-year degree programs instead of gaining career-oriented training that would allow them instant access to the workforce. This inefficiency is increasing student debt and widening a middle-skills job gap, where students fail to meet the needs of employers who want to hire them.

Like their white-collar counterparts, employers in middle-skilled career fields want their applicants to be job-ready. They do not want to have to spend large amounts of money training their employees. They want an employee equipped with both practical and relevant theoretical knowledge. That's where hybrid (or "blended") learning approaches come into play, allowing students to combine in-class hands-on instruction with online learning, contributing to increased productivity among students and reduced costs for institutions.

Penn Foster is helping to close the "skills gap" with a variety of programs that give students access to equipment and first rate instruction in high-growth industries. Our engineering technology program, which prepares students for careers in manufacturing, is just one example. Despite well-documented shifts in the manufacturing industry, there is a dire need for new manufacturing professionals. In December 2012, there were 224,000 manufacturing job openings, but only 155,000 hires, according to the Bureau of Labor Statistics. And these jobs generally pay well: sheet metal workers earn a median salary of $41,710 and diesel engine mechanics earn a median salary of $46,660, according to the Bureau of Labor Statistics. Considering that these careers do not require four years of post-secondary schooling, they represent a favorable return on investment.

Trade and Technical Schools: Meeting the Needs of a Growing Market

The post-high school Trade and Technical Schools industry has experienced overall growth during the past five years despite the recession and substantial cuts in federal funding. The industry has been able to capitalize on the growing online education market, despite increased regulation. Spurred on by demand for training in areas of new technology, revenue grew 2.6% annually to $16.1 billion in the five years leading up to 2012.

Changing labor market requirements have encouraged job seekers to choose vocational courses rather than apprenticeships and on-the-job training. Furthermore, the increasing cost of four-year colleges has caused some to seek alternative forms of education. While technical and trade schools still face competition from the Junior Colleges industry,[10] future prospects are good. Downstream demand is expected to remain strong for workers in most trades, and increasing requirements for workers to hold formal certification will aid industry growth. Demand for healthcare professions will also provide a significant boost to the industry in particular. As the U.S. population ages, demand for medical technicians and nurse's aides will bolster the revenue of training schools, which is expected to increase at an annualized rate of 2.7% to $18.4 billion between 2013 and 2017.

Partnering with Employers, Responding to the Market

Our more than 100-year CTE track record has positioned Penn Foster as the in-demand online and hybrid institution for construction, manufacturing, utility, and engineering firms looking to train and retrain employees. We have partnered with more than 1,000 institutions nationwide in that capacity, including the military. Last year 2,500 military students took Penn Foster programs, because our model allows traveling, busy military families to get an education and advance their career goals and at a low price point. We also work with leading community colleges and corporations to develop turn-key solutions for high-growth industrial occupations such as electrician, welder and HVAC technician, and industries such as utilities, manufacturing and construction.

These programs can reduce employee turnover by 40% while saving corporate clients millions of dollars, not to mention preventing devastating layoffs and improving on-site safety for workers and the public. In addition, they provide traditional blue collar workers with a ladder up into management positions.

This understanding of the job market helps institutions better prepare students to achieve employment. Just as corporate America uses customer data to improve business practices, so do employers collect and track data on performance of employees, interns and apprentices. Schools can harness that data and use it to help students pick classes, decide on courses of study, and ultimately choose their career paths.

Conclusion

The time is now to even better support change in career and technical education in this country and build on the successful foundation in place today. Existing legislation is no longer sufficiently comprehensive to the changing dynamics of today's educational marketplace. Changing the perception of CTE careers, and embracing technology are just a few of the ways that we can positively alter the face of vocational training. We need to focus on training American for the nearly 50% of jobs in the "middle skills" sector that will drive our economy in the years ahead.

Chairman Rokita, Congressman Grijalva, and esteemed members of the committee, we at Penn Foster are looking forward to the challenges and opportunities ahead. Thank you for your time.

ENDNOTES

[1] *http://www.huffingtonpost.com/2013/04/12/growth-online-education-moocs—n—3041529.html*
[2] See Addendum 2 for further information
[3] "Competitive Priority—Improving Cost-Effectiveness and Productivity": *http://www2.ed.gov/about/overview/budget/budget13/crosscuttingissues/pande.pdf*
[4] See Addendum 1
[5] *http://education.stateuniversity.com/pages/2446/State-Departments-Education-VOCATIONAL-EDUCATION.html*
[6] *http://nces.ed.gov/fastfacts/display.asp?id=98*
[7] *http://projectonstudentdebt.org/state—by—state-data.php*
[8] *http://www.propublica.org/article/the-for-profit-higher-education-industry-by-the-numbers*
[9] *http://www.nationalskillscoalition.org/resources/reports/tpib/nsc—tpib—perkins.pdf*
[10] IBISWorld report 61121

Chairman ROKITA. Out of respect for, in order to accommodate as many fellow members as I can, I am going to hold on my questions and go right to members' questions.

So first will be Mr. Thompson. You are recognized for 5 minutes.

Mr. THOMPSON. Well, Chairman, thank you, Ranking Member, thank you for this incredibly important hearing.

And thanks to the panel for your testimony and your experience today.

As co-chair of the Congressional Career and Technical Education Caucus this is a subject obviously I am pretty passionate about. And today we are not just talking about greater opportunities for individuals and families, that is incredibly important, but the big picture is we are talking about America's competitiveness, having a qualified and trained workforce. And the types of programs that you all and the students that you touch, the programs you touch, and the topic we are talking about all serves for America's competitiveness. Career and technical education is not a field of dreams, it is a field of jobs and helping fill that skills gap and make that connection.

First of all, Mr. Chairman, I just want to ask unanimous consent just to submit a statement from my co-chair of the Congressional Career and Technical Education Caucus, a statement from Congressman Jim Langevin.

Chairman ROKITA. Without objection.

[The statement of Mr. Langevin follows:]

Prepared Statement of Hon. Jim Langevin, a Representative in Congress From the State of Rhode Island

Chairman Rokita and Ranking Member Grijalva, thank you for convening today's hearing.

As co-chair of the bipartisan Career and Technical Education (CTE) Caucus, alongside Mr. Thompson of Pennsylvania, I have made the reauthorization of the Carl D. Perkins Career and Technical Education Act one of my top priorities. I am pleased that the committee has taken this important step, and I look forward to working with my colleagues to ensure that Perkins is up to date and fully funded.

The Perkins Act is a major federal funding source for career and technical education in high schools, career and tech centers and community and technical colleges that support professional development, access to the latest technology and equipment, and integration of academic and technical education. Unfortunately, while demand for CTE has increased, funding for the Perkins Act has remained unchanged for almost a decade.

One of the most insidious effects of this stagnation is the ever-growing skills gap: businesses are unable to find employees with the skills to match their job openings, and workers are finding themselves unqualified for the best available jobs. We have some wonderful examples in Rhode Island of partnerships that align workforce training with the needs of employers, but these programs need to be nurtured and expanded. Closing the skills gap is one of the most important things we can do to get our economy moving again, and emphasizing CTE at every level, from elementary school to college and beyond, will help turn out highly-skilled and motivated workers.

High school diplomas are no longer sufficient training for the modern job market. A four-year degree, two-year degree or professional certification is now a key precursor to building a successful and rewarding career. In fact, over 30 percent of the 46.8 million projected job openings by 2018 will require some college education. Meanwhile, eight of top 20 fastest-growing industries in the coming decades will be in the health care industry. Many of these positons will require a 2-year degree or less, but more than a high school education.

Businesses depend on CTE to address the skills gap and shortages of qualified job candidates. They know that CTE students can help meet these demands quickly, and many postsecondary credential and degree programs are available to help students advance. Both short-term and longer-term credentials can be at least as valuable as a bachelor's degree.

In reauthorizing Perkins, I would encourage the committee to build on past successes and to ensure that every student has the opportunity to take CTE courses. Students in CTE classes have better academic motivation, academic engagement, career skills, and overall employability. By connecting classroom experience with real-world achievement, CTE is directly correlated with higher graduation rates.

Money invested in CTE programs is returned back to the economy many times over. In a recent study, the State of Connecticut found that every dollar invested in community college coursework returns $16.40 over the course of a student's career. This translates to a $5 billion per year return to the state. Imagine what we could achieve if such investments were in place on a national level.

Thank you again for convening today's hearing. Perkins has traditionally been a bipartisan endeavor, and I am hopeful that we can continue this tradition moving forward. I look forward to working with my colleagues on the committee to ensure that all Americans have the training to be career and college ready.

––––––––

Mr. THOMPSON. Thank you, sir.

My first question is, one of the key provisions in the current Perkins Act is to focus on programs of study that span secondary and post-secondary education. Have your programs strengthened the secondary/post-secondary connection since the 2006 act was passed? Anyone that would like to field that, please do. Dr. Harrity?

Mr. FISCHER. I could address that first. It has been a lever for change, particularly with getting higher ed to come to the table and secondary ed to come to the table. Not that they were reluctant partners, but we never had a common vision around that. And that provided the common vision. Perkins requires that the post-secondary elements of learning must begin in the secondary ed field, and it was a perfect opportunity, starting with tech prep, to look at articulation agreements and now migrate to real robust dual-enrollment programs. On the industry side, working with businesses, apprenticeship programs that can start in high school and move towards a full apprenticeship license. Things like that have really sprung up since 2006.

Ms. HARRITY. We are very fortunate in Worcester, Massachusetts, to actually have 11 colleges and universities in our city, so we partner and are working very closely with all the presidents and have partnerships. For instance, at our community college, they sent their instructor to our school during our day and certified our allied health students to be EMT certified, and they give our students free of charge seven college credits. They also teach Spanish 1 and 2 during the day, and our students earn six college credits free of charge. In addition, we partner with Worcester Polytechnical Institute where our students actually assisted their engineer students in building a zero-energy solar modular home which they competed in Datong, China, and they actually asked six of our students and two of our instructors to go with them to China for 3 weeks to rebuild the modular home and be part of their competition. So that has been incredible.

Tufts University is in Grafton, which is just about 15 minutes away. They approached us. Our construction students actually built the veterinary clinic that is at our school that has surgical labs and X-ray machines, and we service, with the Tufts veterinary, 250 animals to low-income families couldn't afford proper animal care before.

Mr. THOMPSON. Coming back to the business and industry, because that interface is incredibly important, I believe. That is how we are preparing people for jobs that are there, whether they are emerging industries, industries that are recovering, industries that are just in a transitional phase in terms of the workforce. So in your experience what role does business and industry play in CTE program development and delivery and how can we strengthen that pivotal role?

Mr. Bargas.

Mr. BARGAS. Yes, sir. Business and industry is a critical component in the development of CTE, and we spend a lot of time developing occupational demand, statistics and forecast, so that we can track our technical education programs based upon the demand of the workforce. And our technical college system, our high school system, and our Workforce Commission are intimately involved with this, and we are now providing the path forward to put meaningful CTE programs in place in the State to track the occupational demand.

Mr. THOMPSON. I think I am probably just about out of time, so, Chairman, if I could ask my remaining questions, I will just submit those for the witnesses to be able to respond back in writing, that would be wonderful. I appreciate it. Thank you.

Chairman ROKITA. Without objection. The gentleman yields back.

Mr. Grijalva is recognized for 5 minutes.

Mr. GRIJALVA. Thank you, Mr. Chairman. Let me, if I may, submit for the record, if there is no objection, a statement from the ranking member, Ms. McCarthy, and a statement from the Association for Career and Technical Education.

[The statement of Mrs. McCarthy follows:]

Prepared Statement of Hon. Carolyn McCarthy, Ranking Minority Member, Subcommittee on Early Childhood, Elementary, and Secondary Education

Thank you, Mr. Chairman for calling this hearing to discuss the issue of Career and Technical Education (CTE) Programs. CTE programs, in my opinion, are critical to creating a holistic educational experience for secondary and postsecondary students. As many of us on the Committee understand, curriculums developed with a one-size-fits-all mindset are not effective; and CTE is one example of the type of instructional model that caters to the ever-evolving strengths and interests of students. Especially when CTE programs engage in strategic partnerships with local and national businesses, they can be tremendous gateways to long and fulfilling careers for students.

While CTE programs remain a viable and successful model for students to pursue traditional vocational training, there is a stigma associated with them in that they are considered to be solely for those who do not wish to pursue and attain their four year college degree. However, with soaring student loan debt issues, it must be noted that students are also taking advantage of CTE programs as a means to earn income to help pay for their four year college pursuits as well. To that end, I am proud to note that Nassau Board of Cooperative Educational Services (BOCES), in my Congressional District, offers multiple CTE programs to students, often with college agreements for transferable credit including to our SUNY college campuses.

New York State received nearly $53 million in Perkins IV funding in Fiscal Year 2012 and those dollars seem to be well spent as the State achieved 90th percentile student performance achievements in math and language arts skills. As we discuss the Carl D. Perkins Career and Technical Education Act (Perkins IV) reauthorization, I am looking forward to hearing from our panel of expert witnesses on how we can improve CTE programs going forward, particularly improvements on how it is delivered to students and ways to facilitate program partnerships with businesses.

Thank you, Mr. Chairman.

———

Prepared Statement of the Association for Career and Technical Education (ACTE)

Chairman Rokita and Rep. Grijalva, thank you for convening today's hearing to launch reauthorization discussions for the Carl D. Perkins Career and Technical Education Act. This critical piece of federal legislation is the principal source of funding for career and technical education (CTE) program improvement and is one of the only federal programs that builds the capacity of secondary and postsecondary institutions to offer CTE programs that are academically rigorous and aligned to the needs of business and industry. It is essential to ensuring all students are both college and career ready, as well as to meeting the needs of the country's 21st-century economy. We greatly appreciate your attention on the Perkins Act and CTE more broadly.

The Association for Career and Technical Education (ACTE) is the nation's largest not-for-profit education association dedicated to the advancement of education that prepares youth and adults for successful careers. ACTE has more than 25,000 members from across the country, including career and technical educators, administrators, researchers, guidance counselors and others involved in planning and conducting career and technical education programs at the secondary, postsecondary and adult levels.

Our members have given a great deal of thought to how we might strengthen the federal investment in CTE through the Perkins reauthorization. Our positions, detailed in the attached document, reflect the belief that the purpose of the federal investment in CTE should be clearly focused on ensuring all students have access to high-quality CTE programs in high schools and postsecondary institutions. Perkins should concentrate resources on building a strong system of CTE around the country, beginning early in a student's education with career awareness and broad knowledge and building pathways to more specific career-readiness skills through connections among secondary and postsecondary education and the labor market.

We know that CTE plays a critical role in developing students, with CTE students outperforming their peers on numerous measures of academic and workforce success. The Perkins Act has long been the foundation on which much of this success is built, and we thank you again for your efforts to carefully consider its next reauthorization. We look forward to working with you and the full committee in a bipartisan way as the process moves forward.

The Association of Career and Technical Education (ACTE) is the nation's largest not-for-profit education association dedicated to the advancement of education that prepares youth and adults for successful careers. With that goal in mind, we offer the following recommendations to Congress as conversations begin on the reauthorization of the Carl D. Perkins Career and Technical Education Act (Perkins Act).

Cutting across all of these recommendations must be a clear goal of building the capacity of secondary and postsecondary educational institutions to prepare all students for success in current and emerging in-demand career pathways, which lead to self-sufficiency and provide opportunities for advancement. At its core, career and technical education (CTE) is about preparing a competitive workforce to participate successfully in a global economy—meeting the needs of individuals and employers.

In 2006, the last time the Perkins Act was reauthorized, key progress was made toward these goals, including through the introduction of Programs of Study. CTE student performance results have been positive, and it is critical that the next Act build on current law, by growing the successes and making careful changes to enhance progress.

Priority 1: Redefine the Federal Role in CTE

Since its original authorization as the Vocational Education Act of 1963, the goals of the federal investment in CTE have changed dramatically. While much of this change has been warranted due to evolving education and economic environments, over time the purpose of the legislation has become blurred. With more and more requirements and ideas added to the Perkins Act in each successive reauthorization, it now lacks a clear, consistent focus. As Congress reauthorizes the Perkins Act in the coming years, a close examination of the exact purpose of this legislation should occur.

Key recommendations:

Eliminate multitude of purposes under current law and focus on:
• ensuring all students have access to high-quality CTE programs in high schools and postsecondary institutions
• building a strong system of CTE around the country, which should begin early in a student's education with career awareness and broad knowledge and then build pathways to more specific career-readiness skills through connections among secondary and postsecondary education and the labor market

To support the notion of a strong system of CTE around the country and access for all, ensure that the Perkins Act remain primarily a formula grant designed to support all CTE programs that are willing to make a commitment to high levels of quality and continuous program improvement.

The Basic State Grant federal-to-state and state-to-local formulas should be maintained as drivers of efforts to ensure all students are ready for careers. Technical provisions such as the hold harmless should be updated to ensure equity in funding.

Priority 2: Target Expenditures

As the purpose is redefined and narrowed, so too should funding be more targeted to ensure the most impact on students. Funds should be clearly focused on ensuring programs meet high standards of quality and address areas in need of improvement in order to sustain and enhance student success. Uses of funds within the legislation should be clearer, more exact and fewer in number than in current law. While flexibility for state and local implementation is critical, funding must be linked to the purposes of the legislation and the intended outcomes.

Key Recommendations:

At the state level, better focus state leadership activities on key responsibilities, including:
- strong professional development, at both the pre-service and inservice levels
- leadership development
- curriculum development
- support for local development and implementation of Programs of Study
- stronger connections between secondary and postsecondary systems, including through the development of statewide credit-transfer agreements and data system linkages

At the local level, the current required and permissive uses of funds should be restructured to focus solely on the following areas:
- Providing career exploration coursework and career development activities, career information, and career guidance and counseling to students both before and during CTE Program of Study participation.
- Developing and implementing high-quality Programs of Study, which include coherent sequences of courses connecting secondary and postsecondary education, that are linked to labor market needs and lead to family-sustaining wage, careers. Funding for the implementation of such Programs of Study should be tied to the high-quality program elements described below.

Priority 3: Define Program Quality Elements

In order to ensure that Perkins funding really is targeted to improve CTE programs across the entire education system, a more defined set of quality program elements should be included in the legislation. These program quality elements should focus on essential components that have been shown through prior research to lead to improved student outcomes. Programs should be required to include identified elements, or a plan to implement them, in order to receive Perkins funding, and funding should be targeted to continuous quality improvement of these key areas based on local needs.

Key Recommendations:

Each program funded by Perkins should focus resources on the following elements of high-quality programs, building off the Department of Education's Rigorous Programs of Study Framework:
- Partnerships with business and industry, including required local advisory committees
- Sustained, intensive, and focused professional development for teachers, administrators, counselors on both content and pedagogy to ensure high-quality instruction
- Alignment with rigorous, state-identified college- and career-readiness standards, such as the Common Career Technical Core
- Non-duplicative sequences of secondary and postsecondary courses, including related credit-transfer agreements to facilitate transition between learner levels
- Teaching and learning strategies focused on the integration of academic and CTE content
- Work-based learning opportunities
- Career and technical student organizations, or other activities that incorporate employability skills such as leadership, teamwork, and communication skills
- Appropriate technology and equipment aligned with workplace needs
- Valid and reliable technical skills assessments to measure student achievement, which may include industry-recognized certifications
- Support services to ensure equitable participation for all students
- Strong career development components

Priority 4: Ensure Relevant & Consistent Data

During reauthorization, the Perkins accountability system should be overhauled to ensure fewer and more meaningful measures that are more consistent across states and across federal programs. The system should rely on data that is already available or that can be easily incorporated into state longitudinal data systems to minimize the data burden on educational institutions, and improve and incentivize connections between secondary and postsecondary education and workforce data systems.

Key Recommendations:

Include a small set of core measures that are commonly reported across states.
Ensure that data is collected on key areas of CTE student success, which may include but are not be limited to:
 • At the secondary level: Technical skill attainment, High school graduation, successful post-high school transition
 • At the postsecondary level: Credential attainment, Placement in employment, Postsecondary retention/transfer
Consider the use of indicators for reporting purposes that are not negotiated related to performance and accountability. This reporting should include the disaggregation of data on various student demographic characteristics.
Revise the process for negotiating performance measures to ensure high-performing programs aren't unfairly penalized.

Priority 5: Offer Incentives for Innovation

In addition to the foundational Basic State Grant, the Perkins Act should be a driver of innovation around the country. ACTE proposes a new Innovation Fund, administered at the federal level and modeled after the recent i3 program, to identify and replicate new promising practices within CTE or new and emerging career areas. These funds should be over and above current funding levels and should focus on new ideas that cannot be implemented solely with Basic State Grant funds. Funding should be offered on a short-term basis to launch, but not sustain, programs, and there must be recognition that some innovative programs may not be successful.

Scalability and replicability should be key considerations, with provisions included for the sharing of program results. As an alternative or additional source of innovation, the current reserve fund could be reworked to ensure a stronger focus on new ideas.

Key Recommendations:

Authorize a CTE Innovation Fund as a separate Title within Perkins.
The innovation fund should focus on:
 • funding the identification, development, evaluation, and expansion of new and innovative, research- and evidence-based CTE practices, programs, and strategies
 • funding the development and implementation of career and technical programs of study in new and emerging industries at the regional (or local) level
 • developing rigorous evidence of the effectiveness of innovative strategies on career and technical education student outcomes and CTE program outcomes
 • supporting the rapid development, expansion, adoption, and implementation of tools and resources that improve the efficiency, effectiveness, or pace of adoption of such CTE practices, programs, and strategies.
Funds should be distributed to partnerships of LEAs, area CTE schools, institutions of higher education, and/or postsecondary vocational institutions, as well as other stakeholders.
Maintain the current reserve fund and add new flexibility for states to use the fund to encourage innovative practices. Maintain options for innovative local funding models, such as consortia and the "pooling" of funds among local recipients.

Priority 6: Provide the Infrastructure to Support the System

In addition to direct program support, there are a number of system elements that must be addressed by the federal CTE law in order to ensure high-quality CTE programs around the country. The next Perkins Act should continue a focus on research, evaluation and dissemination targeted toward improving practice. A strong state leadership role should be emphasized to ensure adequate coordination and technical assistance for local systems. Support for data and assessment systems to ensure appropriate program measurement approaches and data linkages, and provisions to address teacher education and recruitment needs are also areas that should be addressed.

Key Recommendations:

Support the continuation of a national research center for CTE focused directly on CTE research, dissemination and technical assistance, particularly in high-priority areas such as teacher preparation and recruitment.

Ensure national activities funds are available to expand and scale-up quality data systems, such as through the creation of national exchanges.

Maintain funding for state leadership and administrative activities, including the state match and maintenance of effort requirements.

———

Chairman ROKITA. Without objection.

Mr. GRIJALVA. And if at this point I would yield my time to Ms. Davis for any questions and comments she might have.

Mrs. DAVIS. Thank you Mr. Chairman.

You have all touched on so many important areas, and thank you so much. I think we often worry about how we can bring things to scale, how we can take the great expertise that comes with principals and with educators in our system and kind of expand those and make sure that they really reach all children with the quality that we are looking for here.

So when we think about those partnerships, and we know we are obviously dealing with what I have always found to be some very, very passionate teachers in this field, and yet what is it that you believe the Perkins Act can do to drive the best in professional education in this area, as well as expanding those partnerships? How would you like to see that? Is it a combination of resources, is it a combination of rewards and grants that highlight the best practices? How do we redo this to make certain that it is getting at what you all have presented today?

Ms. HARRITY. The Perkins Grant is essential for the functioning of our school. For instance, in the biotechnology program our business and industry in central Massachusetts, it was essential that we are creating a pipeline for those jobs. So through Perkins money we actually hired a Ph.D. from UMass Medical School and started a biotech program with the seed money. Since then our district has committed two additional teachers. We had the first graduating class, and our students are all going into STEM majors which is fantastic.

What I would recommend is that there are less requirements for the money in regards to having some more flexibility. A lot of the money is spent on professional development, which is essential for our especially technical teachers to stay current in business and industry expectations, but the ability to use the money in various ways would be very helpful.

Mr. BRITT. I would just add that I think that the Perkins Act does so many important things, but I think there is an opportunity to stimulate innovation in an asymmetrical way by utilizing some nontraditional practices like innovation grants and prizes that would attract not just traditional CTE leaders and innovators to the table, but also people from outside industry. I think that one of the lessons learned across all sectors is you have to harness the best of the talent within a sector, but we live in a world that is more connected, that is more global, and there has to be opportunities for the rest of the non-CTE education world to be part of that conversation. And I think that there are aspects of the Perkins Act that could be directed to innovation and that would I think create complementary perspectives to those that the very seasoned administrators and faculty bring today.

Mr. FISCHER. I would agree with everything that has been stated. I would add that under the current Perkins we use the reserve funds for an innovation grant opportunity and I would hate to lose that. But I would add that what we need to do also is to build more robust data systems and define what data points we are looking at and what defines success. And when we can do that in a more common way across the States, then we can look at informing instructional improvement, providing better professional development, and also engaging with business and industry to say, what is the emerging careers that we need to develop programs for?

Mrs. DAVIS. Yes. Mr. Bargas, did you want to comment quickly?

Mr. BARGAS. I think they pretty well covered the topic in terms of our partnerships we have with public education, as well as our technical college system. I think that pretty well covers the needs.

Mrs. DAVIS. Mr. Fischer, I really do believe, and we have to collect the data, we have to be sure that it is representative of what we are really trying to measure. And how we do that, we would certainly welcome some input about that, because that is critical, and we are never going to get where we want to go, I think, without that.

I think you mentioned in Louisiana the Course Choice, Mr. Bargas, that students have. And I am just thinking how is all that managed? Because in order to have industries using their equipment or engaging students at their sites, which is really the optimum I think we can do, that takes resources, that takes transportation dollars. So how is it that we get there—I see my time is up—but you can———

Chairman ROKITA. The gentleman's time has expired.

We will see if Mrs. Brooks will be recognized for 5 minutes.

Mrs. BROOKS. Thank you, Mr. Chair.

I actually think I know where Congresswoman Davis was going because I am curious with respect to the location issues. As we are looking at reauthorization of Perkins Act, I am curious what you think the most important thing the Federal Government can do to help ensure that all students have access to CTE type of programs. As a mother of a son who graduated from high school a couple of years ago, I wished he had done more CTE programs. I have also been employed with the community college system.

But my point is, going back to more with respect to my son, large public high school, but yet CTE programs are typically located, they are at career ed centers far away from the traditional high school—unless you have a fabulous technical high school, which I love that concept, but not every child is going to choose that. And as they are exploring careers and ideas, if they leave and go off campus for that half a day for those programs they are missing the other college prep and advanced placement type of courses that they need to go to college. So I think we have a very big disconnect between our other academic programs and these academic programs, which people don't call them academic programs, but actually they should be. I think we have huge branding issues, as you have said, with CTE, but we also have these access issues for students who can't go and explore it because then they are getting off the college track.

And I am curious what your thoughts are and if you understand what my frustration is about career programs being located far away from our high schools in separate centers and what should we be doing in the Perkins Act to fix that. Because the programs that CTE offer are fabulous, but not enough kids are getting the opportunity to explore them because they think they will then get off the college track. I would like to hear from all of you. And I love the technical high school programs, but we can't have those everywhere to the exclusion of our other traditional high schools.

Ms. HARRITY. In Massachusetts there are over 60 vocational technical schools, and in Worcester, although we are a career and technical high school, we have our academics, it is a very different model than around the country. We actually have our students in academics 1 week and the opposite week they are in their technical program, then the opposite week they go back to their academics. So we have created authentic learning experiences that are project-based learning. So what we have done to expand that is, because we have been so successful, the comprehensive high schools are now putting in Chapter 74 programs to give the students the opportunity to be part of the experiences for project-based learning.

Mrs. BROOKS. Okay. Outstanding.

Others?

Mr. FISCHER. What a question. Multiple levels of this. So first of all rebranding what career and tech is. It is not my father's voc ed. What it looks like, what it sounds like, and what it produces, the outcomes are big on that, the data plays an important role in that, dual enrollment plays an important role in that. Recognizing that the delivery of CTE can take multiple methods, anytime, anywhere learning, virtual blended learning. Rather than students in many of our areas hopping on a bus every day, we can make better use of virtual and blended learning, for instance.

We can also recognize that some of that learning doesn't take place within the walls of a school, work-based learning experiences. But really saying this is the 21st century programs, they are rich in academics, rich in experience, and heavily backed by business.

Mrs. BROOKS. How would you rename it, rebrand it? I actually think that is part of the problem. Like you mentioned, calling it vocational education I think is taking us back decades and I think it is a huge problem for young people. And so whether it is a comprehensive high school, a tech, I am curious what you all think it ought to be renamed.

Mr. BRITT. Well, two thoughts. First of all, there are 5,000 career academies in the United States, but DOE's definition of a career academy is a school within a school where there is both a traditional school and, whatever the right term is, vocational school. The future model needs to be the technology-enabled career and college readiness academy.

Mrs. BROOKS. Thank you.

Mr. BRITT. It should be "and" not "or." And that is an important distinction. And the project-based learning models that leaders like Dr. Harrity and others are bringing to life actually makes that an "and," not an "or" proposition, because it is an inquiry-based teaching model that allows you to solve problems and it begins to not eliminate the separate disciplines, but it begins to integrate the disciplines into real world, problem solving-based approaches.

As far as the larger issue of branding, in the submitted remarks I did note an example, which is certainly a contemporary one, which is the ''got milk'' campaign. And there is a white space, if you want to put a little marketing parlance, there is a white space available to rebrand this field and own the jobs brand. And I think the opportunity is to bring private sector together, we have a vested interest in an outcome such as this, and really begin to rethink and reposition the brand and the marketing. Just like the ''got milk'' campaign worked——

Chairman ROKITA. The gentlewoman's time has expired. The chair recognizes himself for 5 minutes. Continue on, if you will, please, if you have anything else to add.

Mr. BRITT. My remarks are fine.

Chairman ROKITA. Mr. Bargas, do you have anything to add to Ms. Brooks question?

Mr. BARGAS. To address the issue of facilities and where they are located, we have taken a hard look at identifying high schools across the State that have either mothballed technical labs, whether it be in construction, whether it be in automotive or health care, and working with the technical college system and the other partners we have laid out a plan by which we can go out individually and try to reinvigorate these programs throughout the high schools.

In addition, we have passed a huge bond issue to improve the locations of the technical college system, and we will be doing a lot of new construction. But the key is bringing it back into the high schools and not reducing the rigor of the curriculum, because that is key, and we don't think that that is even a topic for discussion. You have got to keep the rigor, but you have got to offer the technical education as well.

Chairman ROKITA. Thank you for that.

What I am going to do now is read my question into the record. I am going to ask each of the witnesses to respond in writing, if you would. And then I am going to yield the rest of my time to Mr. Grijalva so he can get some questions in.

So the question is, how can the Federal Government support more consistency throughout CTE programs without overburdening State school districts or institutions? So if you wouldn't mind, you have been great witnesses, your opinion is obviously valued, if you could respond to the committee that would be appreciated.

And then with that I yield the remainder of my time, 3 minutes, 20 seconds, to Mr. Grijalva.

Mr. GRIJALVA. Thank you very much.

And one of the questions in writing, in particular to Ms. Harrity and Mr. Fischer, is the impact of sequestration, what has it meant to your high school, and what has it meant to programs in Vermont? And that could be something that the committee can receive in writing.

Let me just, a general question for anybody that wants to answer. As we look forward to the reauthorization of the Perkins Act what is the most important thing the Federal Government can do to help ensure that students have, all students have access to high quality CTE programs, and what are some of the recommendations or some of the ideas that you might have as we go through this process? That is open to anyone.

Ms. HARRITY. My recommendations for the Perkins, I think the grant in itself is very supportive of career and technical education, the vocational school. We are able to use the professional development and buy equipment. If we could be more flexible in the spending. It is really hard to stay in the 21st century with equipment and technology constantly changing. We would be in support of having some more flexibility in regards to the funding stream and where we could spend the moneys.

Mr. GRIJALVA. Mr. Fischer.

Mr. FISCHER. I would add to that creating or ensuring the maintenance of the ability to be flexible and innovative within this. We can follow data once again to look at high-skill, high-wage, high-demand careers, but many times that data only reflects existing industries. We really need to look at the horizon as to what is emerging. And that really takes a concerted effort with business and industry, higher ed, and all sectors of the economy.

Mr. GRIJALVA. Mr. Bargas, and in particular because of the background in your testimony, everybody agrees the importance of work-based training with CTE. I am curious, what are your thoughts about strengthening in this process the role of apprenticeship options for the students in the program that they are studying?

Mr. BARGAS. I am sorry, sir, could you repeat that?

Mr. GRIJALVA. How do you strengthen the use of the apprenticeship program in the course of study for students?

Mr. BARGAS. Currently our program at Associated Building and Contractors includes a 4-year apprenticeship program. And we also have craft training programs. The acceleration of these learning experiences is brought on by the demand from industry and the immediate need for training skilled craft construction workforce.

Mr. GRIJALVA. My time is up. Thank you.

Chairman ROKITA. The gentlemen yields back.

They have called votes. I see no other members requesting to be recognized. With that, we are going to wrap up this hearing. No long speech from me other than just to say a sincere thank you for your leadership in the field. We definitely want to continue working with you. I think on a bipartisan basis we believe in the value of what you do, these programs, and how integral you are, important you are to education in the 21st century, to the success of this Nation in the 21st century.

So again, thank you all for being here. Thank the members for being here. Thank the witnesses for their leadership and their expertise. And we look forward to seeing your answers to the questions posed for the record.

With that seeing no further business before the committee, this hearing is adjourned.

[Questions submitted for the record and their responses follow:]

U.S. CONGRESS,
Washington, DC, November 15, 2013.

Mr. ALVIN M. BARGAS, *President,*
Pelican Chapter Associated Builders & Contractors, Inc., 19251 Highland Road, Baton Rouge, LA 70809.

DEAR MR. BARGAS: Thank you for testifying at the September 20, 2013 hearing on "Preparing Today's Students for Tomorrow's Jobs: A Discussion on Career and Technical Education and Training Programs." I appreciate your participation.

Enclosed are additional questions submitted by members of the subcommittee after the hearing. Please provide written responses no later than December 6, 2013 for inclusion in the final hearing record. Responses should be sent to Rosemary Lahasky or Dan Shorts of the committee staff who can be contacted at (202) 225-6558.

Thank you again for your important contribution to the work of the committee.
Sincerely,

TODD ROKITA, *Chairman,*
Subcommittee on Early Childhood, Elementary, and Secondary Education.

CHAIRMAN TODD ROKITA (R-IN)

1. How can the federal government support more consistency throughout CTE programs without over-burdening states, school districts, and/or institutions?

REP. GLENN THOMPSON (R-PA)

1. As we look toward reauthorization of the Perkins Act, what is the most important thing the federal government can do to help you ensure all students have access to high-quality CTE programs?

2. Realizing that federal dollars are only a small portion of overall CTE funding around the country, how do you use federal resources for CTE in conjunction with state and federal resources? Why is the federal investment in CTE important?

3. What mechanisms of the current Perkins Act have proven most helpful as you seek to continuously improve CTE program quality?

4. One important benefit of CTE programs is helping students make the connections between their traditional academic coursework and real-world application of those concepts. Have your programs been able to align academic coursework with CTE coursework to better help students learn and apply concepts?

Mr. Bargas' Response to Questions Submitted for the Record

DEAR MR. SHORTS, COMMITTEE CHAIRMAN ROKITA AND MEMBERS OF THE COMMITTEE: Again thank you for the opportunity to testify before the Subcommittee on Early Childhood, Elementary, and Secondary Education on September 20, 2013, at the hearing entitled, "Preparing Today's Students for Tomorrow's Jobs: A Discussion on Career and Technical Education and Training Programs."

In response to Chairman Rokita's November 15, 2013 request for responses to additional questions I respectfully submit the following:

QUESTIONS FROM CHAIRMAN ROKITA

1. How can the federal government support more consistency throughout CTE programs without over-burdening states, school districts, and/or institutions?

Funding such as Perkins funding must be allocated such that we invest in high wage, high demand occupations based upon consistent standardized methods of occupational forecasting. States must develop fund sharing partnerships between secondary schools districts, technical colleges, and private training providers to enhance articulation of students course work such that studies from one provider to the other offer more flexibility to the student and accountability to the funding institution.

Funding must require training providers receiving funding such as Perkins to prove that the monies are being spent on high demand training and that training meets or exceeds industry based standards that lead can lead to degree or industry recognized certification without sacrificing rigor in the curriculum.

Also, the federal government can assist in sharing and implementing best practices that occur nationwide, such as responding to social-economic-geographic demand and making technical training partnerships a valued priority.

QUESTIONS FROM REPRESENTATIVE GLENN THOMPSON (R-PA)

1. As we look toward reauthorization of the Perkins Act, what is the most important thing the federal government can do to help you ensure all students have access to high-quality CTE Programs?

First, the federal government needs to ensure that those receiving Perkins funds are spending those dollars in the most effective way. Once again, monies should go to support programs whose standardized curriculum leads to degree or industry recognized certification in high demand high wage occupations and do so without sacrificing rigor and demand. If schools understand they will only get the money meeting these benchmarks, they will do a better job of opening the doors for everyone to get quality CTE.

One of the keys is the active involvement of industry in setting priorities for technical training funding. Louisiana is in year #2 of investing in high wage, high demand, high skill areas and investing in partnerships between private providers and neighboring secondary schools districts and colleges. In Louisiana we share half of the $21 Million between secondary and post-secondary in order to respond to social-economic-geographic demand. We believe this partnering and concentrating of funds towards achieving industry based certifications in our high(est) occupational demand priorities has a greater impact for students and the industries that offer the greatest career opportunities.

2. Realizing that federal dollars are only a small portion of overall CTE funding around the country, how do you use federal resources for CTE in conjunction with state and federal resources? Why is the federal investment in CTE important?

In Louisiana federal funding is leveraged, blended, and invested in conjunction with existing state and industry resources. This holistic approach allows us to best concentrate resources in the names of partnerships with industry. Federal CTE funds and the procedures by which we employ them ensure that funds are invested directly (85%) and indirectly (supporting and administrative 15%) into the classroom . Federal investment in CTE it is an investment that can result in the greatest returns for our country and our states. Students that participate in a quality CTE program graduate at higher rate and they have a head start on a career and training that offer our students the opportunity to achieve their American Dream.

3. What mechanisms of the current Perkins Act have proven most helpful as you seek to continuously improve CTE program quality?

The mechanisms that are most helpful are:
• Encouragements of built-in partnerships
• Mandated collection & reporting of data which allows for analysis and appraisal of performance
• Network of states that sharing best practice
• Mandated investment of Special Populations and Non-Traditional Funding

4. One important benefit of CTE programs is helping students make the connections between their traditional academic coursework and real-world application of those concepts. Have your programs been able to align academic coursework with CTE coursework to better help students learn and apply concepts?

Yes, Louisiana's public education providers of CTE are working harder than ever to expand our partnerships with business and industry groups such as Associated Builders and Contractors, Inc. and state workforce and economic agencies to align our career pathways. For example, selection of high wage, high demand, and high skill areas for partnership are predicated on career pathways. We continue to refine these processes so that colleges/secondary technical education providers can better align with industry standards. This is key to effectively matching our training requirement to achieve industry expectations which ultimately leads to employment in high wage careers.

This important concept should be an everyday occurrence in the academic world. Every course a student takes should emphasize real world application. The programs offered through our high school dual enrollment programs will have core academic classes that are directly related to the career path the student chooses.

I hope the Committee finds the above responses helpful in their work on improving our country's career and technical education opportunities. I would like to acknowledge Robert Clouatre, Associated Builders and Contractor, Inc. Director of Education and Jimmy Sawtelle, Louisiana Community and Technical College System Sr. Vice President for Workforce Solutions for their contributions to my testimony and the above responses for the record.

Please do not hesitate to call upon us if we can be of further assistance.

U.S. CONGRESS,
Washington, DC, November 15, 2013.

Mr. FRANK BRITT, *Chief Executive Officer,*
Penn Foster Inc., 925 Oak Street, Scranton, PA 18515.

DEAR MR. BRITT: Thank you for testifying at the September 20, 2013 hearing on "Preparing Today's Students for Tomorrow's Jobs: A Discussion on Career and Technical Education and Training Programs." I appreciate your participation.

Enclosed are additional questions submitted by members of the subcommittee after the hearing. Please provide written responses no later than December 6, 2013 for inclusion in the final hearing record. Responses should be sent to Rosemary Lahasky or Dan Shorts of the committee staff who can be contacted at (202) 225-6558.

Thank you again for your important contribution to the work of the committee.
Sincerely,

TODD ROKITA, *Chairman,*
Subcommittee on Early Childhood, Elementary, and Secondary Education.

CHAIRMAN TODD ROKITA (R-IN)

1. How can the federal government support more consistency throughout CTE programs without over-burdening states, school districts, and/or institutions?

REP. GLENN THOMPSON (R-PA)

1. As we look toward reauthorization of the Perkins Act, what is the most important thing the federal government can do to help you ensure all students have access to high-quality CTE programs?

2. Realizing that federal dollars are only a small portion of overall CTE funding around the country, how do you use federal resources for CTE in conjunction with state and federal resources? Why is the federal investment in CTE important?

3. What mechanisms of the current Perkins Act have proven most helpful as you seek to continuously improve CTE program quality?

4. One important benefit of CTE programs is helping students make the connections between their traditional academic coursework and real-world application of those concepts. Have your programs been able to align academic coursework with CTE coursework to better help students learn and apply concepts?

Mr. Britt's Response to Questions Submitted for the Record

CONGRESSMAN ROKITA

1. How can the federal government support more consistency throughout CTE programs without over-burdening states, school districts, and/or institutions?

Consistency is important for any successful government program, and we believe a strong foundation for consistency already exists within the US DOE 10 Component framework emphasizing strategies that improve alignment between secondary and postsecondary systems, such as statewide articulation agreements, transcripted postsecondary credit, and stackable credentials. The Framework is viewed by states, school districts and institutions as a guideline that helps create, sustain, and grow Career and Technical Education (CTE) programs. Continuing to review, modify, and update the framework will result in increased consistency throughout CTE programs and improved alignment with industry standards, credentials and overall job market needs.

There are three areas where consistency can be improved:

1. High-quality CTE programs—Federal CTE legislation should focus on promoting excellence in CTE. To that end, the National Research Center for Career and Technical Education (NASDCTEc) believes that more specificity is needed to define elements that are necessary to ensuring high-quality programs. Research by the NASDCTEc underscores our recommendation that federal funding should be delivered through rigorous programs of study, as defined by the Office of Vocational and Adult Education's 10 component framework. The law should emphasize strategies that improve alignment between secondary and postsecondary systems, such as statewide articulation agreements, transcripted postsecondary credits, and stackable credentials. High-quality CTE programs should also expose students to employment and leadership opportunities, for instance, through work-based learning and participation in Career Technical Student Organizations (CTSOs). Federal funds should be distributed only to state-approved, rigorous CTE programs of study.

2. Promote Data Uniformity—Despite significant spending on CTE across the High School, Technical College and Career School sectors, the quality of unit-level and aggregate data on spending and student achievement is often elusive, contradictory, or out-of-date. For example, the basic definition of who and what is a K-12 CTE student varies across states and districts. Is a CTE student a "CTE concentrator" who takes 4-6 CTE courses in one area, or is it any student who takes any CTE course? The definition of what constitutes a CTE course varies across states, districts and even schools. A world-class educational system cannot be modernized without better data and consistency for the sake of benchmarking and performance improvement management on behalf of students and investors. There are substantial private sector innovations in data science that can allow for harmonization without forcing one-size-fits-all. For example, Linked In recently launched University Pages, and around 1,500 schools have already adopted them, helping build visibility to their student bases. The core challenge of that project was successful data harmonization.

Similarly, inconsistencies in how and who provides tracking and reporting costs impact how a given state's delivery system is set up: e.g., New York has a regional service center model (BOCES) that delivers some (but not all) CTE programs for its member school districts. Other states deliver CTE programs in comprehensive high schools. Those variables impact administrative, transportation, instructional, and capital costs.

The government must work to provide a framework for a CTE enterprise that can work as a blueprint and also work to achieve greater data harmonization, data transparency, and fact based results. The lack of data undermines students, employers and governments' ability to maximize the return on CTE investments.

3. Use of Data Dashboards—Use reliable, valid, and educator-friendly "data dashboards" such as the Lexile Framework for Reading and the Quantile Framework for Mathematics to monitor and report on an ongoing basis student progress toward proficiency and preparation for the workforce. The data dashboards use statistically-valid instruments.

CONGRESSMAN THOMPSON

1. As we look toward reauthorization of the Perkins Act, what is the most important thing the federal government can do to help you ensure all students have access to high-quality CTE programs?

The three most important things that the federal government can do are (1) recognize innovative, technology based solutions from both the for-profit and non-profit community to resolve equity issues in both urban and rural environments; (2) reward and provide funding based on—not just CTE enrollments—but on CTE program completion. Some states (e.g., New York) provide a CTE "endorsement" for successful completion of a requisite number of courses in a given career area. The key is a fair reward formula that acknowledges differences, and is not a one-size-fits-all approach; (3) earmark funds for professional development of CTE educators. When educators are able to stay current in their industry, the students benefit.

The federal government should limit the amount of regulatory language in rfps that in some cases shut out the most innovative solutions that come from industry (outside of not-for-profit), and increase regulatory guidelines that favor lowest price submissions in response to rfps. Race to the Top competitive grants are a great example of rfps including language that basically translated the award going to the lowest bidder (e.g. NY curriculum rfp, TN evaluation system rfp, etc.)

The federal government should look at the NASDCTEc recommendation for Innovation funding. The next iteration of federal CTE legislation should allocate new formula funding, above and beyond the basic state grant, to states that incentivize innovative practices and solutions at the state and local levels. Successful innovations should be scaled up using the basic state grant funds.

In short the federal government can be a catalyst for spurning innovation. The assumption that all CTE must be delivered in a ground based school setting is inconsistent with 21st century learning. The reality is that there are many places and ways that students can attain practical experience and career training and those alternatives should be encouraged, whether it takes place online, in actual workplaces or in a traditional school setting.

2. Realizing that federal dollars are only a small portion of the overall CTE funding around the country, how do you use federal resources for CTE in conjunction with state and federal resources. Why is the federal investment in CTE important?

Insist that Perkins funds be used by states in the most effective and efficient ways practical. For example, Effectiveness and Efficiency Framework: A Guide to

Focusing Resources to Improve Student Performance outlines a framework that can be used to:

1. guide schools and districts as to which tools, strategies, professional development, procedures, organization of instruction, etc. they should use

2. serve as a vehicle to compile a national repository of best practices for efficiency and effectiveness

3. guide policy formulation at the district and state levels, based upon #2 above

In the 21st century there is no longer one path for every individual to pursue in education. Alternative pathways, as outlined in the Pathways to Prosperity Report published by the Harvard Graduate School of Education, need to be embraced and encouraged by the federal government. Continued support of the Perkins Act, coupled with new innovations, is a significant market signal to educators and industry alike that CTE remains important.

It is important to note here that districts still heavily rely on CTE federal funding in order to support their programs given the constant challenges tied to local and state budgets—there is local and state funding, but it is not consistent and not appropriated on an annual basis. A key issue in the nation's largest districts is increasing high school graduation rates and providing students with career and/or college ready skills. As school districts carefully examine how to best utilize their local, state and federal funding in order to address both critical issues, it is important to understand the importance of CTE federal funding because it can only be used for CTE initiatives. CTE federal funding provides a critical foundation for districts to prioritize effective CTE programs that would otherwise not exist if it weren't for Perkins funding.

3. What mechanisms of the current Perkins Act have proven most helpful as you seek to continuously improve CTE program quality?

Programs of study are the best way to continuously improve. They incorporate secondary and postsecondary education elements into a coordinated, non-duplicative progression of courses leading to an industry-recognized credential, certificate, or degree. This allows for career schools like Penn Foster to continuously improve our programs of study through reviewing our framework and making necessary adjustments based on employer needs that align to better outcomes for our students.

4. One important benefit of CTE programs is helping students make the connections between their traditional academic coursework and real-work application of those concepts. Have your programs been able to align academic coursework with CTE coursework to better help students learn and apply concepts?

While not funded under the Perkins Act, Penn Foster's collaboration with Job Corps is just one example of a commitment to education innovation in career technical training with students who have struggled in the traditional system. Both Penn Foster and Job Corps are focused on bringing professional and educational opportunities to at-risk students and those who have not had success in the traditional system. Penn Foster operates in 60+ of Job Corps' 125 centers around the nation, implementing a self-paced high school model and devising various innovative hybrid courses that combine online instruction with hands-on training. Since 2006, the partnership has worked by combining general high school requirements such as math or science with electives in a career track of the student's choice. Run simultaneously, Penn Foster provides the materials to help the students receive their diploma, while Job Corps provides them with the practical career training and support. An instructor is present at all times and helps the student decide on and prepare for their next exciting step, whether it's a job or college. When they complete the program students leave with more than just a diploma, they have a skill set that can help lead to a better life.

Given the dynamic nature of the marketplace, it is more important than ever for educators to provide employment-focused education. As students look to train-up and acquire practical and marketable skills, educators must respond in kind by adjusting their methods to be more learner-focused. Ideally, the future of education will blend online and traditional learning experiences and be flexible, so that the material is available to the student on his/her own time and teaching and engagement is saved for the classroom.

Penn Foster's partnerships with businesses provide students with invaluable opportunities to gain practical experience in addition to their education pursuits. For example, in the Vet Tech market we help place students with "hands-on" externships with two of the largest veterinary hospitals in the US: Banfield and VCA. Similarly, we have developed a program that places our Pharmacy Technician students into externships with CVS. These partnerships and others expose our students to the very best that private industry can offer in their fields, while developing the skills they need to find gainful employment soon after completing their matriculation.

————

U.S. CONGRESS,
Washington, DC, November 15, 2013.

Mr. JOHN FISCHER, *Deputy Commissioner,*
Transformation & Innovation, Vermont Agency of Education, 120 State Street, Montpelier, VT 05620.

DEAR MR. FISCHER: Thank you for testifying at the September 20, 2013 hearing on ''Preparing Today's Students for Tomorrow's Jobs: A Discussion on Career and Technical Education and Training Programs.'' I appreciate your participation.

Enclosed are additional questions submitted by members of the subcommittee after the hearing. Please provide written responses no later than December 6, 2013 for inclusion in the final hearing record. Responses should be sent to Rosemary Lahasky or Dan Shorts of the committee staff who can be contacted at (202) 225-6558.

Thank you again for your important contribution to the work of the committee.
Sincerely,

TODD ROKITA, *Chairman,*
Subcommittee on Early Childhood, Elementary, and Secondary Education.

CHAIRMAN TODD ROKITA (R-IN)

1. How can the federal government support more consistency throughout CTE programs without over-burdening states, school districts, and/or institutions?

REP. GLENN THOMPSON (R-PA)

1. As we look toward reauthorization of the Perkins Act, what is the most important thing the federal government can do to help you ensure all students have access to high-quality CTE programs?

2. Realizing that federal dollars are only a small portion of overall CTE funding around the country, how do you use federal resources for CTE in conjunction with state and federal resources? Why is the federal investment in CTE important?

3. What mechanisms of the current Perkins Act have proven most helpful as you seek to continuously improve CTE program quality?

4. One important benefit of CTE programs is helping students make the connections between their traditional academic coursework and real-world application of those concepts. Have your programs been able to align academic coursework with CTE coursework to better help students learn and apply concepts?

REP. RAÚL GRIJALVA (D-AZ)

1. Mr. Fischer, what has been the impact of sequestration on CTE programs in Vermont?

————

Mr. Fischer's Response to Questions Submitted for the Record

CHAIRMAN ROKITA

1. How can the federal government support more consistency throughout CTE programs without over-burdening states, school districts, and/or institutions?

A recent Organization for Economic Co-operation (OECD) report found that while the United States has some of the best Career Technical Education (CTE) programs in the world, the quality of programs throughout the country is often sporadic. The decentralized nature of the CTE system in the U.S. is at once its greatest strength as well as one of the biggest challenges. Current law supports state and local flexibility for how to direct the use of federal funds. This built-in flexibility helps to promote some of the most dynamic and innovative CTE programs in the country and address State specific sector demands. I believe this flexibility for states should be preserved. There is however a few things the federal government can do to support more consistent quality of CTE programs without overburdening recipients of federal CTE funds.

The National Association of State Directors of Career Technical Education Consortium (NASDCTEc) has recently developed the Common Career Technical Core (CCTC), a set of common benchmark standards for CTE. Based on knowledge and skills statements for each Career Cluster(r), these state developed and voluntary benchmark standards incorporate 12 Career Ready Practices, which address the skills and knowledge that are essential to becoming career ready. The CCTC would serve as an excellent method for introducing common expectations into CTE curriculum and programs. This would allow for better comparisons of student outcomes between programs, increase student mobility through improved portability and recognition of credentials, and enhance the sharing of best practices, particularly as students enter a globally competitive economy.

Second, I believe that working toward common measurement and appropriate accountability provisions is necessary. Allowing flexibility in how to achieve the performance goals, as noted above, is appropriate but requiring common reporting would move the system forward.

Finally, the expansion of the reserve fund (currently limited to 10%) would allow states the ability to better promote innovation, scaling up of successful models and rewarding high performance. These flexible resources could further be targeted to help rural or hard-working but low-performing districts and colleges that may receive a very minimal amount of funding through the formula.

MR. THOMPSON

1. What is the most important thing the federal government can do to help ensure all students have access to high-quality CTE programs?

Ensuring equitable access to high-quality CTE programs is, and should continue to be, a priority for a reauthorized version of Perkins. To that end, formula grants provide a baseline of funding to most communities across the country. However, over the last decade the federal investment in CTE has declined precipitously. Increasing the federal investment in Perkins would expand the number of programs and students that could be served. In an era of accountability, we know the Congress is faced with difficult decisions on where to direct limited resources. Perkins is a proven, successful program. Perkins demonstrates a positive return on investment, helping more students graduate high school (when compared to the national average), transitioning more students to postsecondary education and providing students with the skills, knowledge and experience to be well-prepared for today's global economy. Regrettably, the reduction in funding has resulted in programs shutting down across the country at a time when our students, employers and economy need more CTE not less.

2. Realizing that federal dollars account for only a small portion of overall CTE funding around the country, how do you use federal resources for CTE in conjunction with state and federal resources? Why is federal investment important?

The investment the federal government makes in Perkins is ABSOLUTELY essential to the continuation of CTE programs across the country. While the funds have regrettably been cut and their real value diminished over time, the need for these funds couldn't be greater. In some states, the federal Perkins funds are the largest investment in CTE programs. In other states, Perkins is a smaller investment than state funds for CTE. Yet, this does not diminish the role and leveraged purpose of Perkins. Perkins funds incentivize innovation, improvement and focus on needy student populations while State funds many times maintain existing programs. If these funds were to go away, programs and supports and valuable innovation would go away.

Second, federal funds have an express purpose of providing access to CTE programs across an entire state. State and local funds supporting CTE vary significantly in amount but also in how the funds are distributed. In some states, it is the responsibility of the local community to raise funds for CTE programs. This means that the wealthy districts have CTE programs but poor or rural communities go without. The federal funds are essential to ensuring equitable access to high-quality CTE. Right now we are not meeting this mission fully because the federal funds do not go as far as they used to.

Federal investments via the Perkins Act have acted as a catalyst for program improvement and innovation even while those investments account for a smaller portion of overall CTE program funding than that provided by states. Although Perkins funds account for less than 10 percent of all investments in CTE nationally, they remain a driving force behind program innovation and improvement. A recent study by NASDCTEc found that Perkins is the major driver for evaluation and monitoring of the quality of secondary CTE programs and as such, has an impact far exceeding the actual dollars sent to states and locals. Further, the federal funds at the postsecondary level are essentially the only funds the community and technical colleges receive that can be dedicated to program development. Finally, Perkins is the only federal investment that has at its mission connecting and funding secondary and postsecondary programs.

Finally, through the Maintenance of Effort (MOE) provisions and the state match requirements in current legislation, states have been able to use federal funds to leverage additional resources outside of the Perkins Act. This would not be possible without continued federal investment in CTE and is a compelling argument for continued federal investment in CTE.

3. What mechanisms of the current Perkins Act have proven most helpful as you seek to continuously improve CTE program quality?

Currently, the Perkins Act requires states to have at least one Program of Study (POS) in order to receive funding. Programs of Study are an effective tool for ensuring federal funds supports the development of rigorous CTE programs that lead to positive student outcomes. This is accomplished by linking secondary and postsecondary learner levels in a non-duplicative sequence of courses, which ultimately lead to a postsecondary credential or certificate.

Continuing to develop and improve upon the POS model—primarily through the adoption of the U.S. Department of Educations' Office of Vocational and Adult Education's ten component framework for rigorous Programs of Study—will help improve CTE program quality on the whole. We would recommend that all Perkins funds be required to be delivered through comprehensive Programs of Study aligned to regional, state or local economic priorities.

Another useful tool is the reserve fund. By allowing states to focus the reserve fund on priority populations and needs, states have been able to make great advances in preparing students for the workplace and postsecondary education. Increased flexibility in the use of the reserve fund, as well as a greater portion of the funds being allowed to be distributed via the reserve fund would go far to give states the authority to better meet it workforce, economic and student achievement goals.

4. CTE programs help students make connections between their academic coursework and the real-world application of those concepts. Have your programs been able to align academic coursework to better help students learn and apply concepts?

Vermont has made great strides in connecting academic and technical standards and instruction but more can be done. First, we must see the support for this connection between academics and real-world application not only in Perkins but also in the Elementary and Secondary Education Act. Further, supporting competency-based education would allow for demonstration of competency and achievement through real-world projects and activities; and we know that in the real-world you don't separate academic work from technical work—it is seamless.

MR. GRIJALVA

1. What has been the impact of sequestration on CTE programs in Vermont?

The Carl D. Perkins Act of 2006 includes a hold harmless provision that does not allow a state to receive less than the amount they received for their basic state grant allocation in fiscal year 1998. Moreover, current Perkins law incorporates a minimum allocation requirement, commonly known as the "small state minimum", that ensures no state receives less than 0.5 percent of the overall allocation. Both of these provisions found in Title I, Section 111, have had serious complications with the across the board spending cuts, known as sequestration, that were mandated by the Budget Control Act of 2011.

Total appropriations for Title I Basic State Grants under Perkins were reduced by 5.2 percent beginning in July of this year. This amounted in an overall reduction of $59 million in cuts to the national basic state grant allocation. As a consequence, payments to states were proportionately reduced between all state recipients. Perversely, states that have experienced the most growth since 1998, and thus serve a larger student population, have had their state allocations reduced the most drastically because of the interplay between these two provisions. While VT was saved from Perkins reductions using this "small State" clause, other States have seen damaging reductions.

Otherwise, sequestration has had an impact in Vermont on direct services and professional learning opportunities which unfortunately have targeted our most needy students, particularly due to the reductions in IDEA and Title I. Our reports indicate that schools are attempting to manage the financial impact but the burden of essential services has shifted to state resources, at a time when we were least prepared for this added burden.

Some anecdotal information:

1. The total monetary loss to State Title I funds was $1,218,084 or a 3% decrease.
2. The cuts at the LEA allocation level in Title I ranged from 1% to 15%.

3. School Improvement funds were cut by $100,000, approximately 10% reduction.

4. For Title IIA funds, the State allocation was cut by 5.6%. The current total State allocation is $10,199,403 to support statewide professional learning, compared to almost $14 million in FY'09.

Thank you for the opportunity to share these additional thoughts. I am happy to provide additional information or clarification to these questions or other issues that the Committee is considering as it moves forward with the reauthorization of Perkins.

_____

U.S. CONGRESS,
Washington, DC, November 15, 2013.

Dr. SHEILA HARRITY, *Principal, Worcester Technical High School, 1 Skyline Drive, Worcester, MA 01605.*

DEAR DR. HARRITY: Thank you for testifying at the September 20, 2013 hearing on "Preparing Today's Students for Tomorrow's Jobs: A Discussion on Career and Technical Education and Training Programs." I appreciate your participation.

Enclosed are additional questions submitted by members of the subcommittee after the hearing. Please provide written responses no later than December 6, 2013 for inclusion in the final hearing record. Responses should be sent to Rosemary Lahasky or Dan Shorts of the committee staff who can be contacted at (202) 225-6558.

Thank you again for your important contribution to the work of the committee.
Sincerely,

TODD ROKITA, *Chairman,*
Subcommittee on Early Childhood, Elementary, and Secondary Education.

CHAIRMAN TODD ROKITA (R-IN)

1. How can the federal government support more consistency throughout CTE programs without over-burdening states, school districts, and/or institutions?

REP. GLENN THOMPSON (R-PA)

1. As we look toward reauthorization of the Perkins Act, what is the most important thing the federal government can do to help you ensure all students have access to high-quality CTE programs?

2. Realizing that federal dollars are only a small portion of overall CTE funding around the country, how do you use federal resources for CTE in conjunction with state and federal resources? Why is the federal investment in CTE important?

3. What mechanisms of the current Perkins Act have proven most helpful as you seek to continuously improve CTE program quality?

4. One important benefit of CTE programs is helping students make the connections between their traditional academic coursework and real-world application of those concepts. Have your programs been able to align academic coursework with CTE coursework to better help students learn and apply concepts?

REP. RAÚL GRIJALVA (D-AZ)

1. Dr. Harrity, what has been the impact of sequestration on your high school?

_____

Dr. Harrity's Response to Questions Submitted for the Record

CHAIRMAN TODD ROKITA (R-IN)

1. How can the federal government support more consistency throughout CTE programs without over-burdening states, school districts, and/or institutions?

CTE is defined differently in most regions. In certain states CTE is integrated with the academics in other states the students leave the academic school and travel to a CTE center. An animal science program in an urban school district takes on a different set of skill standards than an animal science program in a rural school district. To define a one size fits all standard will not work. Geography, labor work force demands, proximity to post-secondary institutions/business and industry all dictate how a CTE program can prepare students successfully. In my opinion, what worked best for WTHS is increasing academic Rigor for all students (access to Advanced Placement and college courses), increasing Relevancy of why a student is studying/learning/doing a specific task (why a carpenter needs to understand the equation for slope or a cosmetology student needs to know chemistry), improving the Relationships with business, industry, labor unions, and post-secondary institutions so that students have access to much needed internships/co-operative education, hours, and or dual enrollment experiences, and schools have access to those in the fields to help shape and drive current curricula, and also instilling in each student the Responsibility that he/she has to the community that afforded them the opportunity to learn a set of competencies that will lead them to a successful placement (military, post-secondary education, and/or career). I believe that the federal government should require targeted outcomes to ensure CTE consistency through developing common goals (i.e. % of successful placements, academic success, etc.) and through encouraging Rigor (AP and college level courses)/Relevancy (academic and CTE integration)/Relationships (advisory panels)/Responsibility (community service). I don't believe the federal government should design a 'one size fits all' solution.

REP. GLENN THOMPSON (R-PA)

1. As we look toward reauthorization of the Perkins Act, what is the most important thing the federal government can do to help you ensure all students have access to high-quality CTE programs?

Simple—funding. The federal government should continue to fund the Perkins Act and ensure that there is access to the much needed funding to keep programs current in terms of technology and curricula. It takes a lot of money to keep the programs running in a capacity that will prepare a student with the technical competencies to compete in the job market. Many of these competencies require access to the latest technologies whether it is a CNC machine, 3D printer/scanner, tablet, or a spectrometer. Funding should be available to supplement the state funding. Also, many of the Massachusetts CTE programs have a waiting list. This would indicate that more programs or space is needed. Funding is required to expand existing schools or build new ones to accommodate this demand.

2. Realizing that federal dollars are only a small portion of overall CTE funding around the country, how do you use federal resources for CTE in conjunction with state and federal resources? Why is the federal investment in CTE important?

Federal funding is used to supplement the local budgets. These dollars provide access to much needed instructional/technical supplies. It also is used to provide professional development to staff that keeps them current in their field. The monies are also used to help struggling students with support and access to after school programs and or career/college planning. Federal investment in CTE is not only important but it is critical to support the infrastructure of the United States. These dollars are helping students prepare to be successful in their chosen careers and or college. By ensuring students have access to CTE programs and are learning relevant skills, the workforce will have access to skilled labor subsequently keeping business industry from going outside the country to design/produce/sell its wares.

3. What mechanisms of the current Perkins Act have proven most helpful as you seek to continuously improve CTE program quality?

I believe the most useful mechanism for Perkins is the ability to use the funding to start new CTE programs that meet the local and state needs for business and industry. A very successful example at our school was the ability to start a Biotechnology program with Perkins money. The money was used to hire a teacher to design a program that aligned curriculum to biotechnology business/industry needs. The program, in five short years, has expanded to three staff and sixty students. All of the biotechnology students in the first graduating class had 100% successful placement in the biotechnology field. In addition, UMASS Medical School in Worcester, MA just gave us an $825,000 donation to fund the expansion of this successful program. This would have not been possible without the seed money from Perkins.

4. One important benefit of CTE programs is helping students make connections between their traditional academic coursework and real-world application of these concepts. Have your programs been able to align academic coursework with CTE coursework to better help students learn and apply concepts?

Yes, absolutely our students have made this connection. We have worked diligently to provide time and resources to both the technical and academic instructors to work collaboratively on integration projects that bring the two together. Our annual science fair is composed of projects relevant to a students' technical area of study—one example is an early childhood education student worked with a design and drafting student and a machine tool technology student to design an educational toy for pre-school aged children. The design received a patent. Additionally each summer, instructors (academic and technical) are encouraged to participate in an externship with a local entity (business/industry) to learn what it takes to be successful. They then bring this newfound knowledge back to the classroom in the form of updated/relevant curricula.

REP. RAUL GRIJALVA (D-AZ)

1. Dr. Harrity, what has been the impact of sequestration on your high school?

At WTHS, we have not felt the impact of sequestration. However, we know that it has impacted our city as a whole and we anticipate that the ripples will eventually reach us.

———

[Additional submissions for the record from Chairman Rokita follow:]

September 20, 2013.

Hon. TODD ROKITA, *Chairman;* Hon. CAROLYN MCCARTHY, *Ranking Member, Subcommittee on Early Childhood, Elementary and Secondary Education, U.S. House of Representatives, Washington, DC 20515.*

DEAR CHAIRMAN ROKITA AND RANKING MEMBER MCCARTHY: Thank you for holding today's subcommittee hearing on "Preparing Today's Students for Tomorrow's Jobs: A Discussion on Career and Technical Education and Training Programs." The Independent Electrical Contractors (IEC) appreciates this subcommittee's attention to the need to improve access to and emphasis on career and technical education and training in primary and secondary schools. We respectfully submit the following comments for the hearing record, which represent our thoughts on this matter.

I. The electrical contracting industry needs to fill good paying jobs

IEC is a national trade association representing more than 3,000 merit shop electrical and systems contracting companies employing over 100,000 individuals across 56 chapters. Electrical workers are well paid, with the median income of electricians being over $48,000 per year.

The industry is recovering and the demand for electricians is up. However, our current workforce is reaching retirement age and many electricians left the industry during the recent recession. We are having difficulty finding the qualified individuals we need to fill those positions. Projections by the Bureau of Labor Statistics (BLS) indicate that our industry's growing shortage may rise to a deficit of over 150,000 workers by the year 2020.

II. IEC is a longstanding leader in educating the next generation of qualified, successful electrical workers. But, entry level workers must be properly prepared

The electrical industry is highly technical. Contractor personnel have to be able to conduct complex circuit calculations, read and interpret complex technical specifications and building codes, evaluate field conditions, and command knowledge of basic physics, mechanics, and environmental issues to design and install workable electrical systems. Electricians must have advanced education, which a four year college degree does not provide. They must have a strong K-12 education and obtain specialized training. Such training can be provided through an unstructured program of study through a community college or trade school, or through a rigorous U.S. Department of Labor Registered Apprenticeship program such as is conducted by IEC.

In order to successfully enter an electrical education program—either through a registered apprenticeship or through community college or trade schools—students must possess several important qualities.

Entry-level students must have a strong grounding in STEM subjects including basic and applied mathematics through at least Algebra I and basic physical sciences, as well as proficiency in reading and analytics. Further, they must have received basic life skills training and basic employability skills training.

Successful candidates must be able to conduct some physical tasks, such as climbing ladders and lifting at least 50 pounds on a regular basis. They must be mechanically inclined and able to work with their hands. And, most importantly, they must be interested in pursuing a career in the electrical industry and be willing to take direction and learn.

IEC's electrical education program is equipped to provide students with the advanced education necessary.

III. High schools must increase their emphasis on building basic STEM and employability skills to prepare students for both college and career entry.

Unfortunately, our education system is myopically focused on preparing students for a four-year college degree. As a result, far too many leave high school without basic STEM education, life skills, and employability training. We are concerned that our system is so focused on churning out college graduates that high schools have excluded teaching the basics necessary for life and for any occupation. On a national basis, we see young people coming in our educational program requiring significant remediation to bolster their basic math skills and reading. At the same time, high schools have cut funding to labs, workshops, and applied learning programs. Students are leaving school with limited mechanical ability and technical skills necessary to pursue many successful careers.

IEC firmly believes that advanced education takes a variety of forms—and is not limited to a college degree. In fact, IEC is a believer in lifelong learning. Nationally, IEC's registered electrical apprenticeship education program has been evaluated by American Council on Education (ACE) and is recognized for 37 semester hours towards college credit. At the local level, a number of IEC chapter educational programs have individually negotiated articulation agreements with local community colleges. IEC also strongly supports the Registered Apprenticeship-College Coalition recently established by Departments of Education and Labor as a stepping stone for people that want to continue on in their quest for lifelong learning.

We believe that schools need to increase their emphasis on education for a career, rather than education for the sake of college preparation. The education system needs to recognize that a four-year college is not the best investment for every individual. High school education should be broad enough to provide a pathway to either college or the skilled trades. Perhaps most importantly, high school teachers and advisors need to make students aware of all career options available to them, recognizing that students will likely hold multiple jobs over their working career and will need to pursue lifelong learning.

IV. The path forward will require both sufficient funding investments in our nation's education system and support from both public and private partnerships

A July 2013 report by the Urban Institute entitled "Innovations and Future Directors for Workforce Development in the Post-Recession Era" highlights the need for the establishment of career pathways, industry-recognized credentials, work-based learning approaches such as apprenticeship, the need for soft skills training, and the need for establishment of partnerships between government and industry designed to address these needs. IEC believes such partnerships are absolutely critical in supporting career and technical education. SkillsUSA and 4H are two examples of important skills-building organizations that teach professionalism and self-pride while also preparing students for careers in highly technical trades such as electrical contracting.

Further, the decision by many schools to eliminate their career and technical education programs is often cost-driven and skewed by incentives to drive students to college. Lab facilities and equipment used to train students in technical skills require dedicated space, unlike traditional multipurpose classrooms. Reauthorization of the Perkins Act and increased appropriations for career and technical education programs in schools is undoubtedly integral to improving the skills-building and training offered at the high school level. In order to build the skills and the workforce that our industry needs, sustaining both Perkins and Workforce Investment Act (WIA) funding is necessary—further, support for one should not be to the exclusion of the other.

IEC has many more recommendations for improving partnerships between training programs and institutions such as community colleges, which we would be happy to provide in greater detail to this subcommittee.

V. Conclusion

In closing, the focus of our nation's K-12 system needs to be redirected in a way that ensures students are adequately prepared with the basic academic education, life skills, and employability training needed to enter post-secondary education regardless of the specific career path they choose. As part of this, IEC strongly supports Career and Technical Education (applied learning) not only for those individuals that may not be suited for college but for those that preselect a technical career path, and to teach rising graduates integral basic life and employability skills.

Sincerely,

ALEXIS MOCH, *Vice President,*
Government Affairs Independent Electrical Contractors.

September 19, 2013.

Hon. TODD ROKITA, *Chairman;* Hon. CAROLYN MCCARTHY, *Ranking Member, Subcommittee on Early Childhood, Elementary and Secondary Education, U.S. House of Representatives, Washington, DC 20515.*

DEAR CHAIRMAN ROKITA AND RANKING MEMBER MCCARTHY: On behalf of the 140,000 members of the National Association of Home Builders (NAHB), I would like to submit this letter for the record and commend you for having this timely hearing on this all-important topic: "Preparing Today's Students for Tomorrow's Jobs: A Discussion on Career and Technical Education and Training Programs." Through the Home Builders Institute (HBI), the workforce development affiliate of the NAHB, we are dedicated to the advancement and enrichment of education and training programs serving the needs of the housing industry.

For more than 40 years, HBI has trained and placed thousands of youth and adults for careers in residential construction, ensuring that America has a skilled workforce today and for the future. HBI offers a range of Workforce Training and Employment programs to help at-risk youth, ex-offenders, veterans and women train and find jobs in residential construction, serving more than 2,500 in 20 states. One of the most successful programs is HBI Job Corps, which is a national training program that is implemented locally, using proven models that can be customized to meet the workforce needs of communities across the United States. These programs prepare students with the skills and experience they need for successful careers through pre-apprenticeship training, job placement services, mentoring, certification programs, textbooks and curricula. With an 80 percent job placement rate for graduates, HBI Job Corps programs provide services for disadvantaged youth in 73 centers across the country.

HBI also administers more than 120 NAHB Student Chapters throughout the United States, representing more than 3,000 students from high schools, career and technical schools, community colleges and four-year colleges and universities. These chapters enrich the educational experience of students enrolled in construction-related courses through community projects, NAHB chapter participation and guest speakers.

In turn, HBI hopes to create a closer partnership between the educational system and our industry. We are continuing to seek opportunities to expand the existing foundation between school officials and our industry, as the education system considers the offering of more vocational/technical trades programs in school curricula.

HBI, through NAHB, appreciates the opportunity to describe our industry's tremendous investment and commitment to the workforce training of the nation's youth.

Sincerely,

JAMES W. TOBIN III.

———

[Additional submission of Mr. Bargas, "Building Louisiana's Craft Workforce," may be accessed at the following Internet address:]

http://www.laworks.net/Downloads/PR/WIC/
CraftWorkforceDevelopmentPlan20130617.pdf

———

[Presentation submitted by Mr. Bargas follows:]

[Louisiana Craft Workforce Development Board Presentation, October 2006]

Recommendations for Confronting the Skilled Construction Workforce Shortage in Louisiana

The Mission

The Louisiana Craft Workforce Development Board will be a single voice for craft workforce development in Louisiana.

The Goals

• Ensure appropriate focus is given to craft workforce development by contractors, users, government leaders, government agencies, and learning institutions.

• Foster cooperation and communication between public and private entities engaged in craft workforce development.

• Develop a consistent approach to recruiting, training, and retaining a skilled and productive Louisiana craft workforce.

Preamble

The recognized shortage of craft workers in the construction, maintenance, and repair industry is not a new phenomenon in Louisiana.

Although industry experts estimate that they have struggled with workforce development issues for 20 years, the problem has taken a dramatic turn for the worse in the wake of hurricanes Katrina and Rita.

Industrial labor requirements were already trending up sharply prior to the disasters, and this trend has been exacerbated by disaster recovery and rebuilding.

Studies by the Construction Labor Research Council show a national need for 185,000 new skilled craft workers per year during the period 2005 to 2015.

This need for additional workers is being driven by increased demand and replacement of workers leaving the active workforce.

Residential, commercial, utilities, heavy construction, highways, and industrial projects in the state of Louisiana are reaching unprecedented levels post-Katrina/ Rita.

McGraw-Hill estimates that the state will need more than 90,000 new trained craft workers over the next five years.

The Occupational Forecasting Conference predicts that some construction occupations will grow by over 50% in the next four years as a result of recovery-related work.

Contractors are attempting to complete projects with an inadequate number of skilled workers, and this is causing significant increases in project duration, overtime, and installation costs.

Public and private entities, industry associations and labor organizations have come together to address these critical needs by forming the Louisiana Craft Workforce Development Board.

1. Recommendations for Owner Companies, Local User Councils, and Owner Associations

Owners must take the lead to drive workforce development in the construction, maintenance and repair industry. The most effective and long-lasting improvements in the industry are changes that are supported and encouraged by the owner community, similar to the advances in safety over the past 20 years.

Local user councils such as the Greater Baton Rouge Industry Alliance (GBRIA), Greater New Orleans Business Roundtable (GNOBR), Lake Area Industry Alliance (LAIA), and Southwest Louisiana Construction Users Council (SLCUC) function as forums through which contractors, engineering firms, and local owners (users of construction or maintenance services) can address local issues affecting construction, maintenance, and repair.

Owner Companies

The Louisiana Craft Workforce Development Board believes that owners must:

• Establish expectations for workforce development in recruitment, assessment, training and retention.

• Do business only with contractors who invest in workforce development.

• Make contractor commitment to workforce development a factor in the prequalification process. Owners should require a detailed description of the contractor's workforce-development program, including:

• The contractor's investments in workforce development.

• Specific methods used to assess skill proficiencies, along with current skills assessment results for the contractor's entire workforce.

• Documentation supporting continuous skill upgrade and improvement.

• Reserve a certain number of positions for craft workers enrolled in active training.

• Support standardized training curricula, performance standards, and certification, such as the National Center for Construction, Education and Research (NCCER) initiative or equivalent national initiatives that include assessment and credentialing.

• Support the development and implementation of regional and local craft-training programs by placing construction, maintenance, and repair decision-makers on local user councils.

• Actively support contractor, contractor-association, and organized-labor programs that enhance the image of careers in construction, improve the recruitment of entry-level applicants, and increase worker retention.

• Work with owner associations to develop and participate in programs that measure workforce-development effectiveness in improving safety, quality, and productivity. Support award programs that recognize excellence in contractor workforce development.

Local User Councils

The Louisiana Craft Workforce Development Board believes that local user councils must:

• Work with associations and labor organizations in the delivery of workforce development initiatives.

• Encourage members to make contractor commitment to workforce development a factor in the prequalification process.

Local user councils should encourage members to require detailed descriptions of contractor workforce-development programs, including:

• Contractor's investments in workforce development.

• Specific methods used to access skill proficiencies, along with current skills-assessment results for the contractor's entire workforce.

• Documentation supporting continuous skill upgrade and improvement.

• Encourage members to do business only with contractors who invest in workforce development.

• Support standardized training curricula, performance standards, and certification, such as the NCCER initiative or equivalent national initiatives that include assessment and credentialing.

• Actively support contractor, contractor-association, and labor-organization programs that enhance the image of careers in construction, improve the recruitment of entry-level applicants, and increase worker retention.

• Work with area owners, contractors, and associations to assess skilled craft worker availability by trade on a continuing basis, and to develop short- and long-term projections for regional craft needs.

• Work with contractor associations to develop programs that promote the accomplishments of the construction industry and publicize their contributions to the community and state.

• Actively participate with local contractor associations in partnering with area school systems to:

• Promote employment in the construction, maintenance, and repair industry as a rewarding career choice.

• Implement career-education curricula that have articulation with technical and community colleges, ABC Training Centers, and other accredited training institutions.

• Develop programs that measure workforce-development effectiveness in improving safety, quality, and productivity. Develop award programs that recognize excellence in contractor workforce development.

Trade and Professional Associations

The Louisiana Craft Workforce Development Board believes that organizations such as the Louisiana Association of Business and Industry (LABI), Louisiana Chemical Association (LCA) and Louisiana Chemical Industry Alliance (LCIA), and the Louisiana Midcontinent Oil and Gas Association (LAMOGA), must:

• Make workforce development a priority through core values and political action.

2. Recommendations for Contractors, Contractor Assoc., & Labor Organizations.

Contractors and their associations are responsible for workforce development. Recruiting, a demonstrated commitment to training, and worker retention are contractor responsibilities. As an integral component of workforce development, efforts must be made to improve the image of the industry and to educate the public about careers in construction, maintenance, and repair.

Contractors

The Louisiana Craft Workforce Development Board believes that contractors must:

• Implement workforce-development programs that include recruitment, assessment, training, career paths, and retention.

• Work with contractor associations, government entities, and user groups to address workforce-development issues.

• Utilize nationally certified programs such as the NCCER initiative or equivalent national initiatives that include assessment and credentialing.

Invest in training curricula, such as the NCCER initiative or equivalent standardized curricula, correlated to assessment and credentialing.

• Develop and implement programs that are designed to improve retention of skilled craft workers and include clearly delineated career paths, competitive wages, and benefits such as affordable healthcare, transferable healthcare, and portable retirement plans.

- Participate in programs that measure workforce-development effectiveness in improving safety, quality, and productivity.
- Partner with local school districts to inform administrators, school board members, students, parents, teachers, and counselors about career opportunities and educational requirements for construction, maintenance, and repair.
- Participate in recognized industry programs that enhance the image of careers in the construction, maintenance, and repair industry.
- Utilize the Louisiana Virtual One Stop (LAVOS) database to help identify people available for work.

Contractor Associations

The Louisiana Craft Workforce Development Board believes that contractor associations, including Associated Builders and Contractors (ABC), Associated General Contractors (AGC), and the Louisiana Homebuilders Association, must:

- Encourage their members to commit to workforce-development programs that include recruitment, assessment, training, career paths and retention.
- Educate existing and potential members about the importance of workforce development.
- Collaborate and participate in recognized industry programs that enhance the image of careers in the construction, maintenance, and repair industry.
- Partner with local school districts to educate administrators, school board members, students, parents, teachers, and counselors about careers and educational requirements for the construction, maintenance, and repair industry.
- Maintain and enhance current delivery methods to train and certify craft workers throughout the state.
- Encourage the development of innovative craft-training delivery methods that meet the changing needs of the industry, such as lab training, computer-based training, satellite and distance-delivery training.
- Continue to support standardized training curricula, assessment, and certification, such as NCCER or equivalent national initiatives.
- Work with owners to develop and encourage participation in programs measuring the effectiveness of workforce development in improving safety, quality, and productivity.
- Encourage contractors to utilize the Louisiana Virtual One Stop (LAVOS) database to help identify people available for work.

Labor Organizations

The Louisiana Craft Workforce Development Board believes that labor organizations must:

- Support the joint participation of labor and management in apprenticeship training, encourage employer contributions to these activities, and measure the return on such investments.
- Continue to support standardized training curricula, assessment, and certification, such as NCCER or equivalent national initiatives.
- Encourage the development of innovative craft-training delivery methods that meet the changing needs of the construction industry, such as lab training, computer-based training, and satellite and distance-delivery training.
- Participate in recognized industry programs that measure workforce-development effectiveness in improving safety, quality, and productivity.

3. Recommendations for Public Entities

Governor

- Governor's Office of the Workforce Commission
- Departments of the Executive Branch

Labor, Economic Development, Social Services, Education, and Corrections

- The Board of Elementary and Secondary Education (BESE)
- Department of Education
- Local School Boards and Districts
- Louisiana Community and Technical Colleges System (LCTCS)
- Board of Regents
- Legislature

57

Entities Represented

Contractor Entities

Associated Builders & Contractors, Pelican Chapter Industrial Specialty Contractors, LLC
Edward L. Rispone, Chairman of the Management Board
Associated Builders & Contractors, Pelican Chapter Southwest Area
Shaw Group, Inc.
Allen M. McCall, Operations Manager
Louisiana Associated General Contractors, Ken Naquin, Executive Director
Louisiana Home Builders Association, Michelle Babcock, Lobbyist

User Group Entities

Lake Area Industry Alliance, Larry DeRoussel, Executive Director
Greater Baton Rouge Industry Alliance
James Watkins, Contractor Operations Leader, The Dow Chemical Company
Greater New Orleans Business Roundtable, Steven R. Springer, Executive Director
Gulf Coast Workforce Development Initiative
Tad E. Page, Project Mgr-Contractor Communications, Shaw Stone & Webster
Southwest Louisiana Construction User's Council, Larry DeRoussel, Executive Director

Labor Organizations

South Central Laborers Training & Apprenticeship Fund, Gary Slaydon, Administrator/Director

Public Entities

Board of Elementary and Secondary Education, Linda Johnson, President
Louisiana Community & Technical College System, Jim Henderson, Senior Vice President Workforce Development & Training
Louisiana Department of Labor, Girard J. Melancon, Special Assistant to the Secretary
The Louisiana Workforce Commission, N.A. "Pete" Darling, Employer Liaison
Louisiana Department of Education, Patricia Merrick, Career & Technology Section Leader
Louisiana Department of Education, John Birchman, Career & Technology Education (Industrial)

Acknowledgements

Advantous Consulting LLC, Tim Johnson, Partner
Associated Builders & Contractors, Pelican Chapter, Alvin M. Bargas, President, Melanie B. Searles, Director of Administration, Dr. James Owens, Director of Workforce Development
Associated Builders & Contractors, Bayou Chapter, Ronnie Scott, Director of Education
Gulf Coast Workforce Development Initiative Team, Tim Horst, President
Beacon Construction Company
Louisiana Department of Education, Patrick Nelson, T & I Program VITE Certification
Louisiana Department of Public Safety & Corrections, Whalen Gibbs, Assistant Secretary
Louisiana Department of Public Safety & Corrections, Kim Barnette, Education Specialist, Office of Adult Services
National Center for Career Construction Education & Research
Gay St. Mary, Workforce Development Director, Business Roundtable Gulf Coast Training Institute

Facilitator

SSA Consultants
Christel C. Slaughter, Ph.D.

———

[Additional submissions of Mr. Fischer follow:]

Recommendations for the Reauthorization of the Carl D. Perkins Career and Technical Education Act

The Carl D. Perkins Career and Technical Education Act (Perkins) supports Career Technical Education (CTE) programs by strengthening connections between secondary and postsecondary education, aligning to the needs of the economy, and improving the academic and technical achievement of students who choose to enroll in these programs.

The National Association of State Directors of Career Technical Education Consortium (NASDCTEc) believes that the federal investment in CTE legislation, Perkins, should be strengthened by re-examining and re-framing the law to ensure equitable access to high-quality CTE programs of study and to better position CTE to help build the solutions needed to close the skills gap and improve student achievement. Therefore, NASDCTEc believes that federal CTE legislation needs a clearer focus and that its purpose should be ''to develop the academic and CTE skills of students to ensure America's global competitiveness through programs of study, partnerships with employers, and further education and careers.'' These recommendations seek to accomplish this purpose and promote innovation, accountability, and equitable access to high-quality CTE that meet the needs of our nation's students and employers.

Global Competitiveness

• Link CTE to labor market—States are in the best position to determine how CTE can meet the demands of their state and regional economies. Federal CTE funds should only support high-quality CTE programs of study that meet two or more of the following criteria: high wage, high skill, high demand, or high growth. Definitions of these terms should account for varying state and regional economic conditions and labor market needs.

• Rigorous standards—Consistent, quality benchmarks for students in CTE programs of study, regardless of where students live or which delivery system they use, are essential. Federal CTE legislation should require all CTE programs of study to align to rigorous content standards that are national in scope, are informed by the needs of the workplace, and ensure excellence. NASDCTEc believes that federal CTE legislation should encourage state adoption of rigorous college- and career-ready standards, such as those found in the Common Core State Standards and the Common Career Technical Core.[i] Increased consistency and rigor in CTE programs of study will better equip students with the knowledge and skills necessary to thrive in a global economy.

• Innovation funding—The next federal CTE legislation should focus on improving student outcomes through innovative approaches and programmatic improvement. The next federal CTE legislation should allocate new formula funding, above and beyond the basic state grant, to states to incentivize innovative practices and solutions at the state and local levels. Successful innovations should be scaled up using the basic state grant funds.

Partnerships

• Partnerships with business and industry—Strong partnerships between the CTE community and business and industry are essential to high-quality CTE programs of study. Federal CTE legislation should require local advisory committees comprised of employers and education stakeholders who will actively partner to design and deliver CTE programs of study and provide assistance in the form of curricula, standards, certifications, work-based learning opportunities, teacher/faculty externships, equipment, etc. States should have the flexibility to structure local advisory committees in a way that best meets the needs of their state (in terms of governance, funding, geographic and other influencing factors).

• Consortia—Coordination and collaboration between secondary and postsecondary partners is essential and must be improved. The federal CTE legislation should incentivize consortia of secondary and postsecondary eligible entities to better facilitate coordination and transitions between learner levels. States should have the flexibility to structure consortia in a way that best meets the needs of their state in terms of governance, funding, and geographic factors.

Preparation for Education and Careers

• School counseling and career planning—Comprehensive counseling, including career and academic counseling, should be expanded and offered no later than middle school. Federal CTE legislation should provide greater support for career coun-

---

[i] National Association of State Directors of Career Technical Education Consortium, Common Career Technical Core, *http://www.careertech.org/career-technical-education/cctc/*

seling, including all students having an individual learning plan that includes the student's academic and careers goals, documents progress towards completion of the credits required to graduate from their secondary program, and indicates the requisite knowledge, skills and work-based learning experiences necessary for career success. These plans should be actively managed by students, parents, and school-level personnel and should extend into postsecondary education to ensure successful transitions to the workplace.

Programs of Study

• High-quality CTE programs—Federal CTE legislation should focus on promoting excellence in CTE. To that end, NASDCTEc believes that more specificity is needed to define elements that are necessary to ensuring high-quality programs. Research by the National Research Center for Career and Technical Education [ii] underscores our recommendation that federal funding should be delivered through rigorous programs of study, as defined by the Office of Vocational and Adult Education's 10 component framework.[iii] The law should emphasize strategies that improve alignment between secondary and postsecondary systems, such as statewide articulation agreements, transcripted postsecondary credits, and stackable credentials. High-quality CTE programs should also expose students to employment and leadership opportunities, for instance, through work-based learning and participation in Career Technical Student Organizations (CTSOs). Federal funds should be distributed only to state-approved, rigorous CTE programs of study.

Research and Accountability

• Accountability measures—Strong accountability measures are critical to demonstrating CTE's positive return on investment. The current CTE performance indicators should be re-evaluated to ensure that they provide the feedback necessary for program evaluation and improvement, as well as document CTE's impact on students' academic and technical achievement. Federal CTE legislation should require common definitions and measures across the states, as well as allow for alignment of performance measures across related education and workforce programs.

• Research and professional development—Research and evaluation are important guideposts for directing practitioners toward effective practices and guiding state decisions on CTE. Federal CTE legislation should support the continuation of a National Research Center for Career and Technical Education to support CTE educators and leaders through leadership development, quality research, professional development, dissemination, and technical assistance.

State Leadership and Governance

• State flexibility—States should have the flexibility to determine the allocation of funds between secondary and postsecondary education. Funding should be awarded to a single eligible agency as defined in current law. Additionally, states should be given the flexibility to use the reserve fund to implement a performance-based funding system.

• State administration and leadership—Strong state leadership is critical to ensuring that states have the data systems, standards, and partnerships to oversee the development and implementation of high-quality CTE programs of study. Adequate resources for state leadership and state administration, including maintaining the state administrative match, are necessary to ensure effective program administration and equitable access to high-quality CTE programs of study.

The National Association of State Directors of Career Technical Education Consortium (NASDCTEc) represents state and territory leaders of CTE through leadership and advocacy that supports an innovative and rigorous CTE system that prepares students for both college and careers. CTE State Directors lead the planning and implementation of CTE in their respective states and these recommendations reflect their priorities.

[ii] Shumer, R., Stringfield, S., Stipanovic, N., & Murphy, N. (2011, November). Programs of study: A cross-study examination of programs in three states. Louisville, KY: National Research Center for Career and Technical Education, University of Louisville. *http://www.nrccte.org/sites/default/files/publication-files/nrccte—pos—crossstudy.pdf*

[iii] U.S. Department of Education, Office of Vocational and Adult Education, "Career and Technical Programs of Study: A Design Framework." The 10 components are: (1) legislation and policies, (2) partnerships, (3) professional development, (4) accountability and evaluation systems, (5) college and career readiness standards, (6) course sequences, (7) credit transfer agreements, (8) guidance counseling and academic advisement, (9) teaching and learning strategies, and (10) technical skills assessments.

For more information, please contact the National Association of State Directors of Career Technical Education Consortium 8484 Georgia Avenue Suite 320, Silver Spring, MD 20910, 301-588-9630 *www.careertech.org*

———

[Additional submission of Mr. Fischer, ''Reflect, Transform, Lead: A New Vision for Career Technical Education,'' may be accessed at the following Internet address:]

http://www.cciu.org/cms/lib4/PA01001436/Centricity/Domain/148/
New_Vision_Paper_SS12-18-10.pdf

———

[Additional submission of Dr. Harrity follows:]

WORCESTER TECHNICAL HIGH SCHOOL

Laying the Foundation for Future Success

February 9, 2010, marked the 100th year anniversary of Worcester (MA) Technical High School. The school opened as Worcester Boys' Trade High School on February 9, 1910, with 52 student ironworkers and woodworkers attending on weekdays and Saturday mornings—the beginning of vocational education in Massachusetts.

The philosophy of Milton P. Higgins, the school's founding father, was, "To make a good living; to have a happy family; to make preparation for hard times; to wear overalls in the shop with the same dignity as good clothes are worn on Sunday; to be confident that you are laying a sure foundation for any future success; to feel that you are master of your work and that you share the creative spirit; that is the wholesome philosophy of learning a trade." That philosophy holds true today.

In August 2006, what was then

Worcester Vocational High School was transformed into Worcester Technical High School and moved to a new $90 million, 400,000-square-foot facility. Although the demographics of the city and technology and workforce demands have changed, the school's charge remains essentially the same: "to educate and prepare our students, both academically and technically, to meet the challenges of a global society."

Worcester Tech has 1,400 students in 24 technical programs within four small learning communities: Alden Academy, Coghlin Construction Academy, Health/Human Services Academy, and IT/Business Academy. It is the largest of seven high schools in the City of Worcester, and its students are 51% female and 49% male.

Worcester Tech has met adequate yearly progress (AYP) goals for all four years, exceeding benchmarks in English, mathematics, and every subgroup, including special education. The graduation rate for the class of

2008–09 was 85.4%, and the school's drop-out rate was 4.2%, outperforming the district and state in all subgroup populations for graduation and dropout rates. It is a special source of pride at Worcester Tech that no African American students have dropped out.

The school has achieved significant gains in Massachusetts Comprehensive Assessment System (MCAS) scores. In 2009, mathematics and English scores continued to increase in the advanced/proficient categories and the failure rate decreased. For example, as 11th graders, 78% of the class of 2011 scored in the advanced/proficient categories in English/language arts and 70% in mathematics compared with 26% and 34% three years earlier.

Worcester Tech enrolls increasing numbers of students in honors or AP courses. The reasons for those increases are multifold, beginning with the Jump Start program, a three-day program that students attend in the summer before freshman year. Jump Start introduces them to the larger campus and to academic and technical opportunities, student services, and student life and students complete an individual career assessment and begin their personalized career plan. This program is continually modified to meet the students' needs and the school's goals. In 2010, a Tech Scholars piece was added to the program to include honors and AP courses.

By state law, advisory boards must be established for each technical area. The boards must include industry partners, higher-education students, parents, and teachers. In consultation with the general advisory chair, the board makes recommendations for technical curricula, equipment purchases, student outcomes, and continuing education and employment opportunities.

The general advisory board solicits and establishes entrustments, which provide the school with continually updated equipment and technology. The entrustment leases have garnered attention and support from national

WORCESTER TECHNICAL HIGH SCHOOL

pared to compete successfully in the 21st century workforce. It is important that each of the vocational areas address relevant technical skills and in doing so, prepare students to enter not only the world of work but higher education as well." One visit to this school verifies that "The School That Works" is not just a motto but also a daily reality at Worcester Tech.

PREPARATION AND MOTIVATION

Principal Sheila Harrity has held many roles in public education, including teacher and assistant principal, but she didn't have any experience in vocational/technical education. She candidly discusses how she used her experience, knowledge, and skills to allow an experienced vocational education staff to soar and to guide the recent success of Worcester Tech.

When I had the good fortune to be hired to open the new Worcester Technical High School in 2004, I brought a unique combination of experience, knowledge, and skills with me. The success of our school is the result of many factors, and my contributions are squarely connected to my prior work and experience. The success of our school is the result of our redefining the role of vocational/technical education. In doing so, we have emphasized academic standards, teamwork, and motivation.

My background in a suburban high school prompted me to develop programs with extensive college-preparatory experiences for students and to hold them accountable to high academic standards. The technical components of our vocational programs provided an opportunity to make rigorous programming relevant

and international organizations and companies.

The school also employs a cooperative education coordinator who oversees the placement of eligible senior students in paid positions with industry partners. In addition, the coordinator also qualifies students for placements in internships or externships within the community and provides job placements for students and alumni.

All stakeholders are justifiably proud of the progress Worcester Tech has made in a short period of time. Within days of opening the new facility, the staff dubbed it "The School That Works," which suggests the traditional role of vocational education to prepare for the world of work, but means much more.

According to Principal Sheila Harrity, "Our motto signifies that our school must work to meet the needs of our students as members of a global workforce. The needs of the workforce have changed in recent years and the face of vocational/technical education has changed with it. Our school must meet the needs of students to be preto our students. Each of our vocational programs examined its offerings to ensure that students were being exposed to cutting edge technologies and methods. In our academic programs, we redoubled our efforts to simultaneously prepare students for the demands of the state testing program and for college preparation. We closely mapped our curriculum to align it with the state standards and increased the academic rigor of all our programs. The number of honors-level courses doubled, and we have implemented AP courses. Worcester Tech is one of two vocational/technical high schools in the country to receive national and state funding to implement AP courses. Currently we have 125 AP students, a number that will certainly grow as our program continues to develop and more courses are offered.

Redefining academic standards has been integral to our students' success, but our emphasis on teamwork and motivation is just as important. My experience as a college athlete has contributed to my belief that teamwork and proper motivation are important components of student and school success. All important decisions in our school are made by the instructional leadership team, which includes me, the assistant principals, the vocational/technical director, and the department heads in the academic and technical areas.

The team works together to identify focused goals and targeted professional development and to develop a school culture that is marked by high expectations for teachers and students. The team also makes every effort to coordinate professional development on the basis of intensive analysis of student data. Faculty members use that analysis to develop targeted interventions for students and respond to the high expectations of our school

culture by becoming and remaining experts in their content fields.

Finally, I believe that motivation is important for student and staff success. When I was a basketball player at Providence College, I never ran onto the court without a pregame talk from a coach who provided inspiration and motivation to win. Much of what we do at Worcester Tech draws on this lesson from the world of sports. For example, two weeks before students sit for the state exams, the entire student body and faculty take a field trip to a local historical theater to hear a speaker who has overcome personal adversity address students about the importance of overcoming obstacles and reaching personal potential.

Such events are the cornerstone of our school's effort to address the needs of our students and the challenges that they face as residents of our city. The reforms that have been undertaken in our school give students the vehicle they need to take them to a successful life. This assembly program and our school's general focus on the importance of student success provide them with the motivation.

LEADING A CULTURAL SHIFT

The instructional leadership team at Worcester Technical High School provides strong leadership. Many team members were at the school to see the remarkable turnaround with the opening of the new facility and the hiring of a new principal in 2006. When quizzed about the most significant accomplishments at the school over the last five years, the team was able to paint a very clear picture of how these successes came about.

Worcester Technical High School
WORCESTER, MA

Principal
Sheila Harrity

Grades
9–12

Enrollment
1,383

Community
Urban

Demographics

White	51%
Hispanic	34%
Black/African American	10%
Asian/Pacific Islander	4%
American Indian	1%
Free or reduced-price meals eligible	65%
Special education	20%
English language learners	6%

Note: Demographic data are from Spring 2010.

The mission of Worcester Technical High School is to educate and prepare our students, both academically and technically, to meet the challenges of a global society.

WORCESTER TECHNICAL HIGH SCHOOL

Keeping Up in a $90 Million School

Although Worcester Tech's 400,000-square-foot physical plant and structures are extraordinary, they need to be regularly updated with the very latest technology and equipment. A plan to do so was devised by Edwin B. Coghlin, Jr., chairman of the general advisory board: "We started a program called 'entrustments,' in which we would partner with a business, a manufacturer, or a major supplier, and that supplier would provide its equipment, its expertise, its knowledge into the school," he explained. "In return, we would give that particular supplier exclusivity as far as use of the products." It was a groundbreaking strategy that had not been previously implemented at any trade school.

After months of selling this innovative concept, Coghlin and other staff members were able to persuade more than 30 companies to partner with the school. Some were major national brands, a number were small local entities, and still others were foundations, but they all had one thing in common: dedication to the success of Worcester Tech and this new approach. Within the five-year renewable entrustments, the companies place their cutting-edge equipment in the school and advise teachers as they instruct students in its proper use. In return, the school, in its role as a conference and training center, provides a place for the companies to train current employees and sales staff and perhaps identify future workers. The result is a win-win situation. The school has ongoing access to state-of-the-art equipment and techniques each year, and the businesses are able to bring prospective clients to the school for a firsthand look at the latest innovations. As they enter the workforce, graduates will be skilled in using the sponsors' latest tools and technology and may be more likely to use those tools and products on the job.

WTHS Small Learning Communities

Alden Academy
Automotive Technology
Automotive Collision
Drafting
Electromechanical Technology
Machine Tool Technology
Welding

Coghlin Construction Academy
Carpentry
Electrical
HVAC/R
Painting and Decorating
Plumbing and Pipefitting
Sheet Metal

Health/Human Service Academy
Allied Health
Cosmetology
Early Childhood Education
Environmental Technology
Horticulture
Veterinarian Assistant

IT/Business Academy
Business Technology
Culinary Arts
Financial Services
Graphic Communications
Hotel/Restaurant Management
Telecommunications

A change in facility and leadership moved the traditional trade school physically, technically, and intellectually into the 21st century.

The most significant accomplishments of Worcester Tech are considerably intertwined with one another. The major gains in student achievement, the changing culture of the school, the extensive use of technology, and the community perception of technical education have all positively affected student success.

A change in facility and leadership moved the traditional trade school physically, technically, and intellectually into the 21st century. The school's mission, philosophy, faculty, and students remained essentially the same, but the new building's design incorporated four student-centered small learning communities with state-of-the-art technology, communications, and equipment. The days of leaking pipes and roofs; no power, heat, or phones; and crossing a six-lane highway between classes were gone, and the focus could return to education. The new principal brought a big picture vision for the school, its students, its programs, and its culture. The possibilities were endless, and the faculty, staff members, and students became rejuvenated and highly motivated.

The most recognized accomplishment is the significant gains in student scores on the MCAS in English/language arts, math, and science. This achievement is the result of a data-driven school improvement plan, directed professional development, integrated academic and technical subjects, and personalized instruc-

tion. The school has met AYP in the aggregate and in all subgroups for four years. Student and faculty attendance are the highest in the district, along with the highest graduation rate and lowest drop-out rate.

Increasing rigor included doubling the numbers of honors classes, offering AP courses, and receiving the Massachusetts Math Science Initiative grant (MMSI) awarded by Mass Insight Education; Worcester Tech was one of two vocational/technical high schools in the country to receive it. New offerings in the technical areas included veterinary tech, biotech, and expanded environmental tech. Technical programs, along with expanded articulation agreements offering college credit in high school programs, all support our goal to offer relevant and rigorous academic and technical educational opportunities.

Each student is required to maintain a career plan that involves course selection; career pathways; and guidance from their counselors, cooperative education coordinator, and technical instructors. The expanded course offerings, counseling, personalization, and increased opportunities have resulted in a student body that continually achieves at higher levels. Worcester Tech's focus on college readiness has resulted in increased student acceptance to two- and four-year colleges and technical schools, offering students a choice of continuing their education, working in their technical area, or both.

A third—and possibly the most challenging—accomplishment has been to initiate a positive change in the school culture and public perception of vocational/technical education. Expectations for higher student achievement have had to keep pace with the sophisticated knowledge necessary to successfully function in many of today's careers.

Modern professionals work in teams, not in isolation. As one travels throughout the school during the day, students and teachers can be observed working together in a variety of activities, such as supporting technology hardware and software through the student help desk; building robots; running the student-operated restaurant; and serving customers in the bank, school stores, and salon. The vision of a school building that is open well beyond the school day is exemplified in the many student activities, sports, adult education, and other academic pursuits that occur during afternoons, evenings, and weekends.

All around, one can observe a sense of belonging to the school community. This culture shift has been recognized by the community and supported by parents and industry partners, and the transformational work has garnered local and national recognition for Worcester Tech as a highly respected educational institution. The accomplishments have replaced the traditional image of a trade school with one that not only produces world-class tradespeople but also academic scholars. PL

[Whereupon, at 10:54 a.m., the subcommittee was adjourned.]

Æ

Made in the USA
Las Vegas, NV
12 September 2021